WEST SUSSEX
PLACE NAMES

Anthony Poulton-Smith

WEST SUSSEX
PLACE NAMES

First published in Great Britain in 2012 by The Derby Books Publishing Company Limited, 3 The Parker Centre, Derby, DE21 4SZ.

This paperback edition published in Great Britain in 2013 by DB Publishing, an imprint of JMD Media Ltd

ISBN 978-1-78091-017-8

Printed and bound in the UK by Copytech (UK) Ltd Peterborough

Contents

Introduction

For years the history of England was based on the Roman occupation. In recent years we have come to realise the influence of the Empire did not completely rewrite British history, indeed there was already a thriving culture in England well before the birth of Christ. When the Romans left our shores in the fifth century the arrival of the Anglo-Saxons was thought to herald a time of turmoil, yet they brought the culture and language which forms the basis of modern England. Later the arrival of the Norsemen saw their influence and the same is true of our place names, the vast majority of settlement names in East and West Sussex are derived from the Saxon/Old English or Old Scandinavian tongues. There are also the topographical features such as rivers and hills which still have names given to them by the Celts of the pre-Roman era.

Ostensibly place names are simply descriptions of the location, or of the uses and the people who lived there. In the pages that follow, an examination of the origins and meanings of the names in West Sussex will reveal all. Not only will we see Saxon and Scandinavian settlements, but Celtic rivers and hills, Roman roads and even Norman French landlords who have all contributed to the evolution, to some degree, of the names we are otherwise so familiar with.

Not only are the basic names discussed but also districts, hills, streams, fields, roads, lanes, streets and public houses. Road and street names are normally of more recent derivation, named after those who played a significant role in the development of a town or revealing what existed in the village before the developers moved in. The benefactors who provided housing and employment in the 18th and 19th centuries are often forgotten, yet their names live on in the name found on the sign at the end of the street and often have a story to tell. Pub names are almost a language of their own. Again they are not named arbitrarily but are based on the history of the place and can open a new window on the history of our towns and villages.

Defining place names of all varieties can give an insight into history which would otherwise be ignored or even lost. In the ensuing pages we shall examine 2,000 plus years of West Sussex.

Anthony Poulton-Smith

Adur

A district name derived through the process known as back-formation came from the name of the River Adur, which itself is a back-formation from the place referred to in a document of the 17th century as Portus Adurni, Latin for 'Adurnos's harbour'. There is little known about this place save for the mention by the poet Drayton. The river was formerly called the Pende in 1301 and earlier still the Shoreham in 1263. Both earlier names are also examples of back-formation and taken from places along its banks.

Albourne

Recorded as Aleburn in 1177, this name is derived from Old English *alor burna* and describes 'the stream where alder trees grow'.

One glimpse of the roof of the Shaves Thatch Inn is sufficient to understand the 'thatch'. While the long straw here will have been shaved, hence 'shaves', this is now frowned upon as not being the traditional method of trimming the straw.

The River Adur.

Aldingbourne

A name documented as Ealdingburnan around the end of the ninth century and as Aldingebourne in *Domesday*. Here a Saxon personal name and Old English *ing burna* speaks of 'the stream asssociated with a man called Ealda'.

Local names include Lidsey, describing 'the well-watered land of a man called Hlydi'; Limmer Pond tells us it was small enough to be leaped; and Nyton comes from *atten eye tun* 'the farmstead at the island or dry area in a wet land'.

Aldrington

Early forms of this name include Eldretune in 1086, Aldringeton in 1200, and as Alryngton in 1280. Here is a Saxon personal name and Old English *inga tun* which describes 'the farmstead of the family or followers of a man called Ealdhere'.

Aldwick

Listed as Aldweye in 1235, there are two possible Old English meanings for this name. Should this be *eald wic* this would be 'the old specialised farm', however, if the first element is a Saxon personal name then this is 'the specialised farm of a man called Ealda'. In both cases the speciality is most likely dairy produce.

The Waverley public house took its name from Viscount Waverley of Westdean. The title may not be recognised, nor perhaps the holder as Sir John Anderson, Governor of Bengal, Lords Privy Seal, Home Secretary, Lord President of the Council, and Chancellor of the Exchequer. However, even those who are much too young to have known World War Two may well have heard of the Anderson Shelter, distrubuted to households all over the land as a personal bomb shelter.

Aldwick village sign.

Angmering village sign.

Amberley

Found as Amberle in 957 and as Ambrelie in 1086, these records show this to be from Old English *amer leah* and 'the woodland clearing frequented by bunting or yellowhammer'.

The Bridge Inn describes its location near a bridge, the Sportsman shows games and activities are played and/or organised within, and the Black Horse is heraldic and one so common, it is difficult to know the true origin.

Ambersham, South

Records of this name begin with Aembresham in 963. Derived from a Saxon personal name and Old English *ham* or *hamm*, this is 'the homestead of a man called Aembre' or 'the hemmed-in land of Aembre' respectively.

Local names include Gosdenheath, from *gos denu haeth* or 'the heathland by the valley where geese are seen'. Gunter's Wood remembers the family of Roger Gunter, recorded here by 1413. Lastly Topleigh tells us of 'the *leah* or woodland clearing of a man called Toppa'.

Angmering

Seen as Angemaeringum at the end of the ninth century and as Angemare in *Domesday*, this is the '(place of) the family or followers of a man called Angemaer' and derived from Old English *inga* and a Saxon place name.

Upper Barpham and Lower Barpham share an origin of *beorh ham* 'the homestead by the hill or mound'. Hammerpot features the suffix *pot* and speaks of 'the hollow of a man called Harman'. Priorleas Farm is a reminder of former owners of this land, the grandly titled Prior of the Order of St John of Jerusalem.

Public houses here are the Spotted Cow, a misleading description of Holstein or Fresian cattle, a breed which is the highest dairy producer in the world. The

Lamb Inn shows a link to the church, these being closely linked for centuries, while the Woodman Arms is a reminder of the importance the woodman once had in the community.

Apuldram

Not seen until the record of Apeldreham in the 12th century, this Old English place name is either *apuldor ham* and 'the homestead by the apple trees' or *apuldor hamm* and 'the hemmed-in land where apple trees grow'.

Croucher's Farm remembers James Croucher, here by 1704. Dell Quay is named for the depression or dell in the Chichester Channel. The origin of the Black Horse public house is probably heraldic, the image common to many coats of arms including numerous families, the goldsmiths of Lombard Street in London, the 7th Dragoon Guards, and a well-known high street bank.

Ardingly

Listed as Erdingelea in the 12th century, this name comes from a Saxon personal name and Old English *inga eah*, referring to 'the woodland clearing of the family or followers of a man called Earda'.

Bursteye Farm is not named after an horrific injury, this is from Old English *biercen stig* or 'the path overgrown by birch trees'. Fullingmill Cottages took their name from the dirty stream on which they stood, in turn named after the mill and the fulling of cloth. What began as 'the path of a man called Pyppa' is marked on today's maps as Pipstye.

Tillinghurst Farm features a Saxon personal name with Old English *inga hyrst* which speaks of 'the wooded hill of the family or followers of a man called Titta'. Wakehurst Place took the existing name of 'the *hyrst* or wooded hill of a man called Waca'. The delightfully named Saucelands really does refer to a condiment, a place where salt was produced and/or stored in medieval times.

The Gardeners Arms public house seems to have begun as a late alternative to agricultural names such as the plough or farmer. Hence this is an invitation for those who worked the land to partake of the refreshment within. The Ardingly Inn is not named for those who live there but an invitation for those nearby, while the Oak uses the prominent marker as a signpost to those seeking a drink.

Arun, River

A name found as Tarente in 725, Ripa de Arundel in 1288, and as Arunus in 1577. This is another of the rivers named from a place; here this example of back-formation is named from Arundel.

Arundel

Domesday records this name as Harundel, later seen as Esburneham in the 12th century. Here three Old English elements, *aesc burna hamm*, combine to refer to this as 'the hemmed-in land by the stream where ash trees grow'.

Locally the names of Rewell Hill and Rewell Wood share an origin in Old French *roelle* meaning 'little wheel' or Old French *ruelle* 'the little road or path'.

Pubs include the White Hart, originally symbolising Richard II but which eventually became a generic term for any pub. The Arundel Arms requires no explanation, except to point out it was named to show the location to those outside Arundel. The Crossbush and Crossbush Lane are derived from a place name of obvious meaning. Known as the 'Lamb of God', Jesus Christ is represented by the name of the Lamb Inn.

The Norfolk Arms Hotel features the crest of the dukes of Norfolk, whose family seat is at Arundel. The Red Lion shows a link to Scotland, this being the crest adopted by John of Gaunt who fathered an illegitimate line which ascended to the throne of Scotland as the Stuarts and came to England with the accession of James VI to the English throne. The Kings Head is a general reference to the monarchy.

A reference to the patron saint of England and his most famous deed is seen in the George and Dragon. Near an access point to Arundel Park, St Mary's Gate public house simply takes an existing name seen in the Cathedral Church of Our Lady and St Philip Howard. The Eagle pub takes an image chosen by many, not only families but countries too.

Ashdown Forest

Records of this name include Hessedon in 1200, Essendon in 1207, Assesdune in 1275, and Essedon in 1284. The modern form is easy to define as 'the hill where ash trees grow', in which case this would come from the Old English *aescen dun*. However, there are two problems here. Firstly, even on paper the early forms hardly fit with an origin for the first element of *aescen*. Also ash trees simply do not proliferate here and there is no evidence to suggest they ever did. The most likely explanation here is a personal name, this giving 'the hill of a man called Aesc'. Yet in the case of both definitions it is very unlikely that this would be the original name.

Ashington

Recorded as Essingetona in 1073, here a Saxon personal name and Old English *inga tun* speaks of 'the farmstead of the family or followers of a man called Aesc'.

Locals will enjoy a drink in the Red Lion public house, still likely the most common pub name in the land. As with many colour/animal combinations, this is heraldic. There are two possible origins here, either this shows a link to Scotland or to John of Gaunt, the most powerful man in England in the 14th century. Gaunt is an anglicised 'Ghent', where this Duke of Lancaster and member of the House of Plantagenet was born. While he never ruled England in name, as the third son of Edward III he exercised his influence over his

World War One memorial, Ashurst Wood.

Road sign, Ashurst Wood.

nephew, Richard II, his male heirs, Kings Henry IV, Henry V, Henry VI, and female heirs Queen Philippa of Portugal and Queen Catherine of Castille and all the subsequent generations. One cannot ignore a particular illegitimate line known by the surname Beaufort, whose line was legitimized by a decree, with the proviso they had no claims on the English throne. However, they were crowned in Scotland from 1437 and thus, from 1603, also England when the two countries were ruled by the House of Stuart. Hence the image of the Red Lion came to Scotland from John of Gaunt.

Ashling (East & West)

Two names with a common origin, here a Saxon personal name and Old English *inga* refer to the '(place of) the family or followers of a man called Aescla'. The additions are self-explanatory.

Frenchland House refers not to a nationality but to a surname, something akin to Frense or Frensh, although this would have originated as 'French'. Mitchbourne is from Old English *mycel burna* 'the big stream'.

At West Ashling we find the Richmond Arms, this is a reminder of the dukes of Richmond, a title now in its third creation and held by a dozen individuals to date. East Ashling has the Horse and Groom, a reminder of the days when horsepower was just that, while the groom showed stabling was available to those travelling.

Ashurst

Seen in a document of 1164 exactly as it appears today, this name is derived from Old English *aesc hyrst* and refers to 'the wooded hill of the ash trees'.

Hawking Sopers can be traced back to 1327 when Stephen le Sopere is named as the falconer of the lord of the manor. Otter's Farm cannot refer to *Lutra lutra*, our most engaging water mammal, for there is no stream here. Hence this must be manorial and was brought here from Otford in Kent.

Ashurst Wood

Listed as Foresta de Esseherst in 1164, this is from *aesc hyrst wudu*, the Old English for 'the woodland of the wooded hill of ash trees'.

The Three Crowns public house features an image of James I of England and James VI of Scotland. The name symbolises the unification of the three countries of England, Ireland and Scotland when he assumed the throne on 24 March 1603. An instant image of May Day celebrations where the locals dance around weaving intricate patterns on the village green is conjured up by the name of the Maypole public house.

B

Balcombe

With the earliest record dating back to the early 11th century where it appears as Balecumba, this is probably derived from a Saxon personal name and Old English *cumb* referring to 'the valley of a man called Bealda'. However, there is a small chance the first element may be *bealu* meaning 'evil, calamity', indeed that would probably be the definition had the tale of such a period in Balcombe's history survived.

Brantridge Park features the Old English element *brant* thus speaking of 'the steep ridge'. The Half Moon Inn has likely retained its popularity through being associated with the night, the time most would frequent the local pub. However, the oldest will have been heraldic, a common device used in many coats of arms. If the modern sign is taken as a copy of the original image, then the crescent moon is shown in her increment (heraldric talk for the horns pointing to the left) on a field azure (a blue background) and would be a late indication of the Balswill family.

It must be said there is no written evidence this family ever had any connection with the area and would seem very unlikely to have been the reason behind the name. However, the exercise is not entirely pointless as it does show the great difficulty in linking a modern unreliable image on the sign to a much earlier family crest. Yet there are no such problems in finding the origin of the Cowdray Arms; this tells us the family name and their seat is at Cowdray House near Midhurst.

Barlavington

Listed as Berleventone in 1086, the *Domesday* record combines a Saxon personal name and Old English *ing tun* and tells of 'the farmstead associated with a man called Beornlaf'.

Barnham

Found as Berneham in 1086, there are two possible meanings for this place name. Should this be Old English *beorn ham* then this would give 'the homestead of the warriors', however, if the first element is a Saxon personal name this would give 'the homestead of a man called Beorna'.

The Barnham Hotel may speak for itself, but to find the origins of the Murrell Arms we need to look at records from 1784 which shows this to be home to William and Elizabeth Murrell.

Beeding (Lower & Upper)

Two places with a common origin, found as Beadingum in the ninth century and as Bedinges in *Domesday*. Here a Saxon personal name and Old English *ingas* describes the '(place of) the family or followers of a man called Beada'.

At Upper Beeding, Horton Hall was built on a region known as 'the dirty farmstead', a reference to the muddy land. Tottington Farm links Old English *ing tun* with a Saxon personal name and tells of 'the farmstead associated with a man called Totta'.

Lower Beeding has Colgate, one of those names which, when defined, paints a picture of life in Saxon times. Two elements here, *col* and *geat*, describe 'the way of the charcoal burners', that being the way into the forest where wood was cut. Charcoal burning involved smouldering wood, stacking the cuts and covering them with earth to ensure the heat was sufficient to remove impurities and moisture without bursting into flame and consuming the fuel. Such involved watching the pile night and day, an extremely boring but necessary task where the charcoal burners were almost guaranteed to fall asleep. Hence they took to sitting on a stool with just one leg so, should sleep come, they would fall from their precarious perch and awaken. This is the origin of the phrase 'to drop off'.

Pubs here begin with the Bridge Inn, no surprise to find it within a few yards of a bridge. The Plough is a popular image since the 16th century, a time when the majority worked the land. A tree growing nearby would act as a marker for the Crabtree.

With no image outside the Kings Head, today it would seem the reference is not to a specific monarch but to royalty in general. However, a photograph from some 50 years ago shows the name on the side of the building as the Old Kings Head. A second smaller sign hangs at the front of the pub with what is certainly an image of a person. However, the grainy black and white photograph is not clear enough to see who is represented. The Rising Sun is an heraldic sign beginning as a representation of Edward III.

Bepton

Domesday's Babintone points to this as coming from a Saxon personal name and Old English *ing tun* and 'the farmstead associated with a man called Bebba'.

Bugshill Lane has nothing to do with insects, this is a corruption of a name speaking of 'the slope of the beech tree wood'. Much as modern developers want to give a suggestion of a rural setting with their suggestions for street names, landlords have always tried to give their premises names pointing to an idyllic countryside location. This is still the case in the Bepton pub called the Country Inn.

Bersted

The earliest surviving record of this name dates from 680 where it appears as Beorganstede. Derived from Old English *beorg ham stede*, this describes 'the homestead by a tumulus'.

What began as 'the *ham* or homestead of a man called Baebbi' is today known as Babsham Farm. Chalcraft Barn was once the independent settlement 'a smallholding where calves are reared'. Elbridge comes from *thel brycg* 'the bridge of planks', where 'th' has been dropped owing to it being confused with the definite article.

Loats Lane is from *hlots* or 'portions', where parcels of land were allotted to the poor. Norrups Barn tells us it is at the northern end of the parish. Finally Shripney, which seems to be Old English *screpan eg* 'the dry land in the marsh which has been scraped clear', although this would be a very rare use of *screpan* as a place name.

Bignor

Recorded as Bignevre in the *Domesday* survey of 1086, this name features a Saxon personal name and Old English *yfer*, telling us it was known for 'the hill of a man called Bicga'.

Billinghurst

The earliest surviving record of this name is as Bellingesherst in 1202. This form is a little late for us to decide whether this is a Saxon personal name and Old English *hyrst* and 'the wooded hill of a man called Billing', or *biling hyrst* 'the wooded hill with a sharp ridge'.

Grainingfold Farm is from a personal name and *inga falod* meaning 'the pen or fold of the family or followers of a man called Graegel'. The same last element is seen in Hadford Farm as 'the pen or fold of a man called Hadda' and in Tedifold 'the pen or fold of a man called Tudda'.

Highfure comes from *heah fyr* literally 'the high fire', probably a marker beacon but written evidence is not available and archaeology will never prove as such. Marringdean Farm tells us it was at 'the woodland pasture near a boundary stone'. Tisserand tells of 'the marshland of a man called Tydi'. Adversane has the suffix *hyrne* referring to 'the corner of land of the Hadfield estate'.

Pubs include the Foresters Arms, a name indicating this was a meeting place of the Ancient Order of Foresters. This friendly society had branches at lodges, also known as courts, across Britain and the USA. When the railways arrived at a place in the 19th century publicans were keen to offer a welcome to travellers in the form of a new pub, perhaps even renaming one, and here we find the Railway Inn.

The Half Moon Inn features an easily recognised image, albeit correctly a crescent moon, and one associated with the evening when pubs are busiest. Naming the Sun Inn may have been suggested by the idea of a rival to the moon, although most often this represents an image of a warm welcome. From the 17th to the 19th centuries Drungewick Manor was home to the Onslow family; they are remembered by the Onslow Arms.

The Blue Ship seems an odd name for a pub so far from the sea. It has been a pub since the middle of the 19th century, although the building dates from the 16th century. While nobody knows the real origins, two suggestions have been put forward. One suggests the building used wood from an old ship for its beams, such recycling was commonplace. While it is not unusual to find the name 'Ship' even further inland, we often find this to be a corruption of 'sheep', the pronunciation little different from Old English *scep*. This seems the most plausible, especially with the Blue Sheep also being an old Sussex breed.

What began as a row of three cottages occupied by those employed to burn limestone in kilns to produce lime, this used as a fertiliser, is today aptly known as the Limeburners Arms. In the case of the Blacksmiths Arms the reference is to the metalworker being situated alongside the inn, the two often worked together to take care of the horse and rider. The Six Bells shows a link to the church, often thought to depict the number of bells in the belfry; it should be noted this is rarely the case.

While the Kings Arms shows support for the monarchy in a general sense, the image outside the Kings Head is obviously that of George III. Both carry the same message, one of patriotism, the latter simply referring to the man who was on the throne at the time. And he reigned for a long time, indeed no king comes close to his 60 years and only two Queens, Victoria and Elizabeth II, surpass his tenure. Sadly his reign is associated with the loss of the American Colonies and his supposed madness. While his doctors were baffled by his condition during his lifetime, today scientific knowledge seems to point to the blood disease porphyria as the cause.

Binderton

Listed as Bertredtone in 1086, as Bendrinton in 1205, Bendreton in 1237, Bynderton in 1279, Bundrit in 1288, and as Binton in 1691. Three elements here, Old English *ing tun* following a female Saxon personal name to give 'the farm associated with a woman called Beornthyrth'.

Locally the names of Preston Farm and Crows Hall Farm refer to 'the farmstead of the priests' and 'the hollow where crows are seen' respectively.

Binsted

The earliest surviving records of this name include Benestede in the *Domesday* census of 1086, Bynstede in a document dated 1296, and as Biensted in a listing from 1332. Here is Old English *bean stede* which describes 'the place where beans are grown'.

The Black Horse public house features an image used to represent the 7th Dragoon Guards, the goldsmiths of London, and numerous families. Hence it is impossible to know the correct origin.

Birdham

A name found as Bridham in 683 and as Brideham in 1086. This is derived from Old English *bridd hamm* or *bridd ham* and giving 'the hemmed-in land frequented by birds' or 'the homestead frequented by birds' respectively.

Minor place names include Batchmere's Farm, 'the pool of a man called Baecci'; Broomer Farm comes from *brom mor* 'the moorland where broom trees grow'; Courtbarn Farm recalls John de Court, here in 1338; Cowdry Farm comes from Old French *coudraie* 'the hedge of hazel'; Lippering Farm tells of 'the place associated with a man called Lippa'; and Manhood End is on the boundary of the hundred called Manhood, itself from *maene wudu* 'the common wood'.

Pubs named the Bell Inn are invariably linked with the church, hence perhaps we should see this as being chosen for its simple but easily recognised sign. This is best illustrated as a silhouette where the bell shape is equally easy to see.

Bognor Regis

The earliest known record of this name comes from the end of the 10th century as Bucganora. Here a Saxon personal name precedes Old English *oru* and describes 'the shore of a woman called Bucge'. The Latin addition, *regis* meaning 'of the king', is very recent and not seen until 1929 when it was officially bestowed on the place following a period of recuperation here by George V. Spencer Terrace here was named after the 18th-century politician Lord Spencer.

While the town was named after a monarch called George, the George Inn most certainly was not. Records of ale being allowed on the site of the present pub date from 1622, almost a century before any George sat on the throne. Hence we know this is a reference to the patron saint of England even before the listing from 1705 as the George and Dragon.

However, the Prince of Wales certainly does refer to royalty, the reference being to the heir to the throne generally and not a specific holder of the title. It goes without saying the Victoria Inn commemorates the monarch who reigned in England for longer than anyone. The White Horse shows a royalist establishment, the name becoming popular when it came to these shores as part of the coat of arms of the House of Hanover. The Royal Oak refers, not to a specific individual so much as an event. Here we recall how Charles II hid in the Boscobel Oak near Shifnal in Shropshire.

Southdowns is a pub name referring to the nearby range of hills. Similarly the Bersted Tavern takes a place name, one meaning 'the place for barley'. Locality is also found in the name of the Beach House, Old Barn Free House, and also the Railway Emporium. A description of the place is found in the Two Way Inn, and the Top House. The Elmer Inn is in Elmer Road, Brewsters is a clear reference to the product, while the Waterloo Inn remembers the battle of 1815.

The Unicorn is of heraldic origin, it represents Scotland on the royal standard. The Wheatsheaf represented the Brewers' Company and also the Worshipful Company of Bakers, many early inn-keepers providing both services to the community. The Friary Arms is on land linked to the church, the same link seen in the Lamb Inn, it being a reference to the Son of God. To find the Ship Inn was almost obligatory for this coastal location.

The sea front at Bognor Regis.

People are marked by the name of the Richmond Arms, honouring the dukes of Richmond, whose family seat is at Goodwood House, near Chichester. The Hatters Inn is after Richard Hotham who made his name, and considerable fortune, as a hatter and hosier and almost single-handedly established Bognor as a resort in the 18th century. The Berkeley Arms is after the family at Berkeley Castle, one of the very few families who can trace an unbroken male line right back to Saxon times. The name of the Martlets is heraldic; it is used to represent the 4th son of a nobleman, and tells us he inherits nothing.

Bolney

A name derived from a Saxon personal name and Old English *eg* and describing 'the dry ground in a marsh of a man called Bola'. This appears as Bolneye in a document of 1263.

Locally we find Chatfields, this name describing 'the *feld* or open land of a man called Ceatta'. Rice Bridge is from *hris* meaning 'brushwood', this being the site of a causeway of brushwood through the wetland area. Colwood is derived from *col wudu* meaning 'the woodland where charcoal burners work'.

Pub names include the Queens Head, more likely to prove a general show of support for the monarchy than a specific queen. The Eight Bells has a delightful sign featuring eight actual bells. There is no doubt this shows the pub is on church land for this is the normal number of bells in a peal.

Bosham

Recorded as Bosanham in 731 and as Boseham in 1086, here is a Saxon personal name and Old English *ham* referring to 'the homestead of a man called Bosa'.

Local names include Colner Farm, this telling of 'the *mere* or pool of a man called Cola'; Creed Farm features *cryde* or 'the place where plants grow'; Walton is from *wealh tun* 'the farmstead of the Welshmen or Britons'.

The Berkeley Arms features the shield of the family whose history is centred on Berkeley Castle in Gloucestershire. This important landholding family have held lands in Gloucestershire since Saxon times. Another, the White Swan, probably features part of another coat of arms. Here the majestic image was adopted by many quite diverse companies and individuals, including the Vintner's Company, the Poulters' Company, the Musicians' Company, the earls of Essex, and Edward III.

With a French element to the name, the Anchor Bleu has a sign with an image of a small fishing boat. A conversation with the present owner revealed records of this place go back to the 16th century and it has been licensed since at least 1708. During all that time the place was known as the Anchor, the addition not seen until the 1940s. Coincidentally this was when Canadian troops were stationed nearby and possibly the reason for the pronunciation *bleu* if not the origin. These premises stand between the harbour and the church, the latter being older and certainly the original holder of the land. Blue is a colour representing Christianity, the Anchor is also used to represent this religion, an idea found in the Bible where in Hebrews 6:19 we find the words of St Paul: 'We have this as a sure and steadfast anchor for the soul, a hope...' that one's faith would prove an anchor in life.

Botolphs

This place name appears as Sanctus Botulphus in 1288; this place is named from the dedication of the parish church to St Botolph.

Annington Farm describes 'the hill associated with a man called Anna', the personal name followed by Old English *ing dun*.

Boxgrove

Listed as Bosgrave in 1086, the *Domesday* record points to an Old English origin of *box graf*, this describing 'the grove where box trees grow'.

Minor names here begin with Crockerhill, telling us it was 'the hill where a crocker (maker of pots) lived'; Goodwood began life as 'the wood of a man called Godgiefu'; Halnaker can still be seen as describing 'the half an acre' of cultivated land; despite its name Seabeach has no connection with the shore but is from 'seven beech trees'; and Strettington refers to the *tun* or 'farmstead of the *straet*' referring to Stane Street.

Bramber

Recorded as Bremre in 965 and as Brembre in 1086, here is a name from Old English *bremer* and describes 'the bramble thicket'.

Maudlin House uses the phonetic spelling of Magdalen College, Oxford, who owned this land.

The Castle Inn Hotel is only 200 yards from Bramber Castle, built soon after William the Conqueror was crowned King of England to defend the port on the River Adur. Although now a ruin, there is more than enough remaining to show this was a substantial building before the pounding by the Parliamentarian forces which reduced it to the ruin it is today.

Broadwater

Listed as Bradewatre in 1086, here the *Domesday* record points to an origin of *brad waeter* and speaking of the '(place at) the broad stream'.

Here Charman Dean takes the name of the family recorded here in 1557. Heene comes from *huin*, literally 'family or household' and thus the sole remaining element of the original name. West Tarring describes the '(place of) the family or followers of Teorra', while the similar Worthing speaks of the '(place of) the family or followers of a man called Weord'.

At Broadwater the Cricketers public house leaves no doubt this was home to a local cricket team.

Burgess Hill

A name not recorded before 1597, when it appears as Burges Hill. While no surviving record of the place name is seen until the end of the 16th century, there is evidence of the Burgeys family being here by the 13th century.

The old working windmill which gave its name to the Windmill public house is still the most obvious feature of the village. The Watermill Inn refers to its location near the river. From the large bale of fleeces transported around the country, and a common sight at inns, comes the Woolpack. The Potters remembers a traditional industry in Burgess Hill, this image is also seen on the shield of the town's coat of arms. The Junction Inn took its name from Junction Road, itself a reminder of the railway junction here, the line also giving a name to the Railway Hotel which offered refreshment to travellers.

Showing a team was based here and played the national summer sport is the basis for the name of the Cricketers. Hogshead takes the name of the large cask used to store and transport wines and beers, the product is also advertised on the sign of the Brewers Arms. The Weald Inn refers to the region deriving its name from 'the high previously forested land'.

The Royal George ensures there is no confusion with St George, the usual origin of pubs named 'George'. The Kings Head is certainly a general show of support for the monarchy, and thus the nation, the unmistakable image of Henry VIII on the sign was chosen as instantly recognisable, certainly not relevant to the age of this pub.

When the businessmen who founded the Mooch@76 pub were trying to think of a different name they were getting nowhere and so one of them sent a text message to a friend looking for inspiration. The text began: 'Hi bud, just mooching around looking for some ideas for a pub name.' This produced the 'Mooch', a slang term for 'looking around' and when added to the address (this is number 76) by the @ used in text speak, they produced the very modern pub name.

This is not the only time alternative terminology has given a pub name. What was officially the Royal Oak was known by the locals as Jacob's Post. This was the name of a nearby post, itself marking the site of a gibbett where Jacob Harris was hanged and left to rot in chains as a warning to others, reputedly the last man in England to suffer such a fate. He was convicted at Horsham Assizes in 1734 and found guilty of three murders.

Burpham

Records of this name include Burhham at the beginning of the 10th century and as Bercheham in *Domesday*. This comes from Old English *burh ham*, this is 'the homestead of or by the fortified place'.

Peppering describes the '(place) of the family or followers of a man called Pipera'. Wepham is derived from 'the *ham* or homestead of a man called Waeppa'.

The George and Dragon public house is named after the patron saint of England and his most famous deed.

Burton

A common place name which is often found with an addition and especially, as here, when it refers to a parish. Yet records such as Botechitone in 1086, Bodeghtone in 1291, Boudeketon in 1314, and Bouketon in 1428 show this name has never had a second element to distinguish it from others. Another surprise here is the origin, for unlike nearly every other example it is not from Old English *burh tun* 'the farmstead of the fortified place'. That this has a very different origin, thus a different evolution, is the reason there is no second element, for it simply was not necessary for much of its life. Here the first element is a Saxon personal name, a derivative of Boda which tells of 'the farmstead of a man called Bodeca'.

Locally we find Skeets Moor, a name which recalls former resident William Skyte.

Bury

Here the name is seen as Berie in the *Domesday* record of 1086, this is Old English *burh* or the '(place at) the fortification'.

Barkhale Wood is from *beorc halh* meaning 'the nook of land where birch trees grow'.

The Squire and Horse Inn is a rather different pub name reflecting the long established link between the horse and the public house. Most simply refer to a staging post or stable where the animal, and of course its owner, could be rested. However, here there is no doubt the mention of the squire can only be a very definite attempt at snobbery, hence suggesting a higher class establishment.

Byworth

Listed as Begworth in 1279, this name comes from a Saxon personal name and Old English *worth* and tells of 'the enclosure of a woman called Beage, or a man called Baega'.

Chichester

This name appears as Cisseceastre in 895 and as Cicestre in 1086, the suffix here is undoubtedly Old English *ceastre*, however, there are two possible origins for the first element. Most likely this is a Saxon personal name and refers to 'the Roman stronghold of a man called Cissa', yet if this is *cissen* it gives 'the Roman stronghold at the gravelly place'.

It comes as no surprise there are numerous street names in Chichester which can be traced back directly to the many of those who have played their part in the history of the cathedral. This selection shows almost all served as bishop. Ashburnham Close remembers William Ashburnham, bishop 1754-97. From 1929 George Bell served, his name remembered by Bell Close. Brideoke Close dates from the 17th century when Ralph Brideoke was bishop. Carleton Road can be traced to 1619, when Bishop George Carleton began his stint of nine years.

Bishop Ashurst Turner Gilbert, his term lasting from 1842 to 1870, is seen in Gilbert Road. Hilary was bishop for 18 years from 1147, Hilary Road is named after him. Langton Road remembers John Langton, who was made bishop in 1305.

Canon Lane, Chichester.

Bishop Luffa Close remembers Ralph Luffa, only the third man to hold this office. Montague Road was named after the 17th century bishop, Richard Montague.

From 1224 to 1245 Ralph Neville was in office, hence Neville Road. Bishop William Otter, who took office for just four years from 1836, is remembered by Otter Close. The Ridgeway is from 1908 when Charles John Ridgeway became bishop until 1919. In 1508 Bishop Robert Sherbourne took office, his name taken for Sherbourne Road. Earlier still, in 1478, Bishop Robert Storey was given the post; he is remembered by Storey Road. Wilson Close takes the name of Bishop Roger Plumpton Wilson. Also St Wilfrids Road, is named after the seventh century bishop.

Those who should be singled out for special mention include Durnford Close; Richard Durnford not elected to office until his 68th year and yet still managed to see 26 years as bishop. John Arundel Road remembers the man who served as bishop 1459–68; he also served as the chaplain to King Henry VII and, earlier still, as the royal physician.

Chichester Priory.

Barlow Road takes the name of William Barlow. Undoubtedly the most controversial of Chichester's bishops, he fought a long battle with the City Corporation over fishing rights of citizens with the harbour limits. Perhaps the most remarkable statistic is revealed by his six children. Just one son, himself going on to become Bishop of Lincoln, and five daughters, all of whom grew up to marry bishops.

Mayors are always a popular source of inspiration for street names. Such a choice is unlikely to prove controversial for, after all, to attain the office of mayor requires years of dedication and hard work for the community. George M. Turnbull was a twentieth century mayor and also the proprietor of a local gents' clothiers. Shopkeeper Arthur Frederick Lewis was in office during the 1920s, hence the name of Lewis Road. Gilmore Road remembers the 1930s and Henry Gilmore Napper, who also found time to run the post office and general stores. Eastland Road remembers Thomas Jesse Eastland and his wife Alice Florence Eastland, the latter the first lady to serve as mayor.

Walls Walk, Chichester.

Not that one has to rise to the office of bishop or mayor to have a road named after you. Sometimes simply living here is sufficient as in the case of George Chatfield, recorded at what is now Chatfield Road in 1586. Manning Road comes from 1600, when fishmonger Edward Manning was in residence. Taverner Place can be traced back to 1249, when William le Taverner was here.

In the early 15th century John Mumford was living at Mumford Place. By 1540 John Castleman was at Castleman Road. We must assume he was a neighbour of Elisha Bradshaw, recorded at what is now Bradshaw Road in 1536. Blandford Road took the name of John Blandford, recorded here in 1545. Greenfield Road remembers the family represented by Richard Greenfield in 1602 and John Greenfield in 1633.

John Barton, merchant and benefactor, gave his name to Barton Road. Oliver Whitby Road remembers the man who founded a school for boys. Barford Road and Whiteside Close recall two men, both doctors, Arthur Barford and Paddy Whiteside respectively. Similarly Douglas Martin Road honors the man who was a renowned surgeon. Hay Road took the name of historian Alexander Hay. Dalloway road took the name of the Reverend James Dalloway, also an historian.

Landowners are obvious choices and have given us Henty Gardens, Farndell Close and Florence Road, although the latter was correctly spelled Florance. Newlands Lane recalls John Newland who, along with his two brothers, all represented England at cricket. Leigh Road took the name of Stephen Leigh, Langdale Avenue is on land held by the Reverend Langdale, and Upton Road took the name of the farming family here.

Lastly two individuals who have streets named after them, who certainly knew one another, and were on very different sides. Juxon Close remembers William Juxon, chaplain to Charles I who is known to have been present at the King's execution and who was rewarded at the Restoration of the Monarchy by being made Archbishop of Canterbury.

Market Cross, Chichester.

We also find Cawley Road, named after John Cawley, a family of brewers and the first of a family who were among the most important in Chichester for several generations. Like Juxon he was also involved in the execution of Charles I but for very different reasons. Cawley was one of those who signed the death warrant. At the Restoration Cawley escaped to Switzerland, where he lived until his death.

Locally we find names such as Graylingwell, from a personal name with *inga wielle* this is 'the stream of the family or followers of a man called Graegel'. Guilden Road tells us this was cut on lands belonging to a guild brethren. The Pallant features the Latin for 'palace', informing us this was land which had palatine rights for the Archbishop.

Rumboldswhyke was held by the Wyke Chapel of St Rumbold, Whyke itself is a place name telling it was held by the Archbishop. Spitalfield Farm is recorded as being a possession of the Hospital of St James. Stockbridge tells us this river crossing was made from 'stocks or logs'.

Pub names of the city begin with the most obvious, those advertising the product. The Barley Mow features a main ingredient of beer, while a 'mow' is simply another word for a stack or sheaf. Labour in Vain may not seem it but is also advertising the product. During the days when inns often brewed their own, here the message is to competitors rather than customers and warns an attempt to reproduce the excellent quality of the ales served within was pointless, that they would labour in vain.

If not offering the product directly, nobody is turned away at the Globe Inn, the message is clear in this is open to all. The Crab and Lobster would have advertised local sea food. Named the Happy Medium is a pub which may well have had evenings where crystal balls, palms and cards are read, however, the message refers to the premises as the best environment to enjoy a chat or conduct business.

Trades could also be said to offer a welcome, either to a prominent local industry or to show that the landlord or owner possibly worked in that trade. The Blacksmiths Arms became popular in the days when the local metalworker would forge a business relationship with the publican. Hurdlemakers is more obscure, this being the temporary fence panels used to pen animals. The Woolpack Inn takes the name of the large bale of fleeces which were used to transport wool around the country using pack animals before the coming of the canals and later the railways.

Both the Nags Head and the Coach and Horses represent transport. Clearly the latter is a reference to the coaching era, while earlier a small but sturdy animal known as a nag (the reference in no way derogatory) could be hired to take the traveller on the next leg of his journey. Effectively both signs represent the historic equivalent of a bus stop or railway station as is the case with the modern name of the Mainline Tavern.

The days of the coaching era may also be the origin for the Hole in the Wall. While their passengers alighted and luggage was unloaded and awaiting those who were joining the route here, the coachmen were passed refreshment through a small hole especially for this purpose. There are many other explanations, including debtor's prisons, where lepers were holed up, and even in the modern era the earliest ATM machines, originally referred to as the hole in the wall.

While it may seem unusual today, names have also been influenced by religion. In times when the vast majority earned their living off the land, the church and the local were the only two places anyone outside family or work colleagues were met. The Mitre is a clear link to the bishops, this being the headgear showing their office. Much more common is the Bell Inn, not only is the message obvious but the shape instantly recognisable. The Hope features an alternative way of referring to one's religious beliefs.

Location and place names themselves are seen at the Chichester, Park Tavern, Eastgate Inn, Wickham Arms, Selsey Bill and Selsey Arms. The Manor House tells us where the premises could be found, while the Bush Inn took its name from a prominent nearby feature. The Four Chestnuts probably began as trees too, although the sign painter has depicted the name as horses. The Thatched Tavern is recognisable by its roof, and the Seal refers to the sealing of the town charter.

Dolphin and Anchor public house, Chichester.

Chichester has long been an important harbour and its links to the sea are clear in its pub names. The Fountain is an image found on the coat of arms of the Master Mariners. No surprise to find the image of a vessel used for the Ship Hotel. The Dolphin and Anchor features two images associated with the sea: the dolphin was considered the sailors' friend while the anchor, as an image, was chosen to represent one's faith. The Crown and Anchor is taken from the arm badge worn by Royal Navy petty officers, possibly an indication of an earlier career of the landlord. The Neptune recalls the mythological god of the sea, while the Lively Lady was opened in 1968, the year Sir Alec Rose completed his own solo voyage of the globe, the second to do so, aboard his yacht *Lively Lady*.

Among those of heraldic origin we find the Bull's Head, a common image for this is a powerful animal and adopted by many families and bodies. Both were used to represent Catholicism, this being the image on the seal of the Pope, hence such edicts being referred to as a 'papal bull'.

Oddly coloured animals are invariably heraldic, although it is not always clear who or what they were intended to represent. Other names duplicate that basic theme, without having real etymological value such as in the case of the Spotted Cow. The Swan may be either an attractive image or have heraldic origins.

On the subject of animals few, if any, communities can have more pub names featuring the fox. The success and adaptability of this mammal has led to pub names through several avenues, such as heraldry, anthropomorphism, surname, or simply an attractive image. Indeed its very popularity is the reason for the name of the Charlton Fox, giving a distinctive addition to a very common name. Fox hunting was clearly not a favourite sport of a landlord or owner of the Fox Goes Free, unlike that of the Fox and Hounds.

Patriotism is seen in the name of the George and Dragon, the patron saint of England is paired with the creature whom he is said to have killed. Royal references are also patriotic and no royal reference is more common than the Royal Oak, a reminder of the escape by Charles II, who hid in the branches of an oak tree at Boscobel near Shifnal in Shropshire, to evade capture by Parliamentarians. The Prince of Wales refers to the title held by the heir to the throne rather than any holder of same.

The Star and Garter also has a story to tell. As the two images associated with the Most Noble Order of the Garter, it was instituted in 1348 by Edward III and

The Fountain public house, Chichester.

limited to the sovereign and just 25 others. It was said to have occurred to him at a court ball when a blue garter fell from the leg of the Countess of Salisbury, widely regarded as the most beautiful woman in the land. Picking it up the King noticed those present eyeing him and quickly slipped it over his own leg announcing *Honi soit qui mal y pense*, now the motto of the order and meaning 'Evil to him who evil thinks'. The story is undoubtedly apocryphal but nevertheless worth repeating.

Individuals who have given their names and images to the signs include Edward Turnour. In the middle of the 18th century he was made 1st Baron Winterton, his seat at Shillinglee showing the link with Sussex.

Imagery was important in times when the vast majority of the population were illiterate. While modern signs will doubtless show a chimney sweep, the real origin goes back to coffee houses when young black men, gaudily attired in a striped uniform, were used as personal servants by the rich. Similarly the Rainbow is a very simple and naturally colourful image and easily reproduced.

A unique idea for a chain of Wild West America-style pub restaurants is seen in the Smith and Western. This does not represent the make of firearm, that was a Smith and Wesson. This was officially known as the Fort Smith and Western Railroad, with a main line extending approximately 200 miles from Fort Smith, Arkansas and Guthrie Oklahoma.

Humour is never far away when pubs are being named. The Slug and Lettuce is now a chain of bars and eateries, not the most attractive image when trying to attract custom. However, this name dates from long ago and is the subject of a somewhat amusing anecdote. Landlords wished to convey the message of the name of the establishment to a clientelle who were largely illiterate, but well-painted signs could prove very expensive. This particular landlord had a reputation for being frugal and thus quickly took up the offer of a neighbour to paint the image for a small reward. When the sign was hung confused locals asked what it was meant to represent. When told it was a cow grazing in a meadow one wit responded that it 'Looks more like a slug and lettuce' and the name stuck.

Chidham

Listed as Chedeham in 1193, this is probably 'the hemmed-in land near the bay' from Old English *ceode hamm*.

Hambrook comes from Old English *hamm brook* describing 'the brook by the water meadow'.

The Bosham public house takes its name from the place which faces it across the tidal estuary and which is defined under its own entry. The Old House at Home became popular in the 19th century when a poem by Thomas Haynes Bayly was set to music, the narrative expressing the thoughts and feelings of a soldier fighting overseas and reminiscing on his childhood and longing again for home.

Chilgrove

A name found as Chelegrave in 1200, coming from one of two Old English origins. Either this represents *ceole graf* and 'the grove in a gully' or, should the first element be a Saxon personal name, then 'grove of a man called Ceola'.

The White Horse Inn is a pub name from heraldry, a representation of the House of Hanover who reigned from 1714 to 1901.

Chiltington, West

The second 'farmstead associated with the slope of the hill called Cilte' which, as with the previous entry features a Celtic hill name with Old English *ing tun*. This name is found as Cillingtun in 969 and as Cilletone in 1086, the addition distinguishes this from its namesake above.

Coneyhurst Common describes 'the wooded hill frequented by rabbits'. Crowell Farm comes from *crawe wella*, 'the stream or spring where crows are seen'.

The Queens Head public house features an image of Anne of Cleves. As the fourth wife of Henry VIII her tenure as Queen lasted in essence for just six months until the annulment. However, she was never crowned queen consort nor, we are assured, was the marriage consumated. Thereafter always referred to as 'the King's beloved sister' she received a very generous settlement which included land around West Chiltington. While the six Mrs Henry-the-Eighths are generally understood to have been unfortunate women whose liaison with the King brought them to an untimely or unfortunate end, this Queen did not sleep with the King, was never required to perform any royal duties, got a nice settlement, and actually outlived the King and the other five wives.

No surprise to find the Elephant and Castle is heraldic, the image of the pachyderm with a howdah on its back was used in the arms of the Cutlers' Company from the early 17th century. The howdah was mistakenly described as a castle, not surprising when very few would have even heard the word, while the association with the elephant chosen for ivory being used for the most exclusive cutlery.

Whilst any reference to a bell is seen as a link to the church, perhaps the Five Bells is an exception. While not on the coast it is quite possible a former mariner could have come here as landlord and suggested the name Five Bells as used at sea to show the time. If so ringing such would refer to 2:30pm, not seen as particularly relevant today but easily seen as closing time for the lunchtime session before licensing laws were changed at the end of the twentieth century.

Chithurst

Records of this name include Titesherste in 1086 and as Chyteherst in 1279. Most likely this represents a Saxon personal name and Old English *hyrst* giving 'the wooded hill of a man called Citta'. However, the first element *ced* or Celtic 'wood' cannot be discounted.

Holmhill is derived from *holegn hyll* or 'the hill where holly grows abundantly'. Pennels Bridge recalls the family of Dominus William Paynel, here by 1296.

Clapham

Domesday's Clopeham from 1086 is the earliest form to survive, this is from Old English *cloppa hamm* and describes 'the hemmed-in place by the hills'.

Michael Grove may seem to be a personal name, however, the true origin is Old English *micel grafe* 'the great woodland grove'.

Public houses here include the Coach and Horses, a pub name showing this is an old coaching inn, effectively the equivalent of the modern bus stop.

Clayton

Listed as Claitone in 1086, here Old English *claeg tun* and describes 'the farmstead on clayey soil'.

Freek's Farm takes the name of the Ferkche family, here in 1332 and transferred from a place name derived from Old English *fyrhthe*. The Jack and Jill public house was named after the windmills on the south downs. Both are still in full working order and themselves named from the nursery rhyme where two children went up the hill.

Climping

Records of this name start with *Domesday*'s Clepinges in 1086, later seen as Clinpinghes in 1194, as Clympininges in 1228, and as Climping in 1260. The only possible origin here is Old English *climp* meaning 'lumpy', however, this simply does not fit with the local topography and thus, especially with the suffix of *ing*, must surely be a nickname. Thus this should be seen as the '(place) associated with a man known as Lumpy'.

Locally we find Atherington, referring to 'the farmstead of the family or followers of a man called Eadhere or Aethelhere'. Cudlow Barn represents a personal name and *hlaw* and tells of 'the tumulus of a man called Cuda'.

Church of St Mary at Climping.

Pubs here include the Oystercatcher, a modern name chosen to reflect the seafood menu as much the coastal location. The Black Horse is a common name most often derived from an heraldic image, although the image is so common it is difficult to see where it comes from.

Coates

Listed as Kotes in 1142 and as Cootes in 1537, here is a name described from Old English *cote* in a plural form. Here then is 'the cottages', however, no mental image of thatched brick buildings, painted pure white with roses growing around the door please. The Saxon cottage would probably be described today as a hovel, with the family living at one end and their animals at the other.

Cocking

Found as Cochinges in 1086, the *Domesday* record is insufficient to show whether this is a Saxon personal name and *inga* giving the '(place of) the family or followers of a man called Cocca' or, if this is derived from *cocc inga* and 'those found at the hillock'.

Bex Copse recalls former resident Daniel Becke, who was here by 1296. Crypt Farm is a rather morbid corruption of Old English *grype* or 'drain'.

No doubt the Blue Bell Inn refers to religion, this colour always represents Christianity.

Coldwaltham

Listings of this name include Uualdham in 683 and as Cold Waltham for the first time in 1340. Three elements here, all from the Old English tongue, which produce quite a lengthy definition. Firstly *ham* is 'homestead', while *weald* refers to 'high forested land now cleared', and the later addition of *cald* tells us this was 'exposed'. Together this describes 'the homestead at the exposed place of the high formerly forested land which has now been cleared'.

The local pub is known as the Labouring Man. This features a disappointingly uncommon double-sided sign inviting two of the workers who would indeed have worked up a great thirst. On one side is a man using a scythe, while the reverse features the blacksmith toiling away at his anvil near the fierce heat of his furnace.

Colworth

First found in the 10th century as Coleworth, here is a Saxon personal name and Old English *worth* giving 'the enclosure of a man called Cola'.

Compton

Listings of this place name include Cumtun in 1015, as Contone in the *Domesday* record of 1086, and as Cuntuna in 1164. A simple enough name to define, this being Old English *cumb tun* 'the farmstead in a valley'. Indeed this is such a common name we do find a distinguishing addition for a short time from the 12th to the 14th centuries. That addition of St John referred, not to the dedication of the church but, to a local family.

The Coach and Horses is an indication this was a stop in the days of the coaching era.

Coombes

Recorded as Cumba in 1073, as Cumbes in 1202, and as Combes in 1265, the Old English *cumb* in a plural form talks of this as the '(place) at the valleys'. While the place occupies only one valley there are several in the vicinity.

From Old English *aeppel hamm* comes the name of Applesham Farm, a local name describing 'the hemmed-in land where apple trees grow'.

Copthorne village sign.

Copthorne

A name which can still be seen as coming from Old English *coppod thorn* and describing 'the pollarded thorn tree'. This place is recorded as Coppethorne in 1437.

Prince Albert public house in Copthorne.

The Cherry Tree public house most likely took the name of a nearby tree. Whilst the cherry could never be seen as the largest species, doubtless in the spring when covered with blossom it would have stood out and made an excellent marker. Another features the image of the consort of Queen Victoria, the man who is generally held to have introduced the Christmas tree to our islands, Prince Albert.

The Hunter's Moon is a surprisingly common pub name as it refers to a single night in the year. The full moon nearest the autumnal equinox is the Harvest Moon, the next full moon being the Hunter's Moon. It is sometimes said to have been named as it produced sufficient moonlight to hunt migrating birds but this seems unlikely as the term was in use well before the gun was used for hunting as a sport. These are the only two full moons given a specific name, this is down to circumstances regarding the orbit of the Earth and tilt of the axis reducing the time difference between moonrise on one day and the next to between 30 and 40 minutes, rather than the usual 50 minutes.

Cowfold

Found as Coufaud in 1232, this early record is easy to see as Old English *cu fald* and 'the small enclosure for cows'.

Locally we find Lydford, from *lad ford* 'the ford of the trackway'. Oakendean has nothing to do with trees, this is 'the pasture for swine of a man called Occa or Ocga'. The name of 'the wooded hill associated with the Britons' from *wealh hyrst* existed long before Wallhurst Manor was built. Woldringfold features a Saxon personal name with *ing falod* or 'the fold associated with a man called Wulfhere'.

A pub known as the Coach House shows this was once a stop on the network of coaching routes which were the main method of transport until the coming of the railways.

Crawley

The earliest surviving record dates from 1203 as Crauleia, a name from Old English *crawe leah* or 'the woodland clearing frequented by crows'.

Shelley Plain comes from Old English *scylf leah*, telling of 'the woodland clearing at the shelf of land'.

Pubs here start with the Black Swan, once used as an image in heraldry to refer to something very precious or rare. The idea behind this being it was thought every swan in the world was white, that was until Australia's native population of black swans were discovered. However, the image of the black swan is still known to represent something very special, which is the message behind the pub name.

Other names having possible heraldic beginnings, including the Black Dog, one where it is difficult to know what or who it represents. The White Hart is another, for while it was first seen as a pub name during the reign of Richard II, it taken from his arms, it remained as common if not more so centuries later. This continued popularity is entirely down to it being used as the generic term for a pub, much the same as the vacuum cleaner is nearly always known as a Hoover.

The Greyhound is almost certainly taken from the coat of arms of the dukes of Newcastle who owned land in many places in England. What is certain is this is the venue for the World Marble Championships. This family also gave a name to the Pelham Buckle, the family name is Pelham and a silver buckle is featured in their arms.

Goffs Manor is one of Crawley's oldest buildings, found on the edge of Goffs Park. The name can be traced back to the family first seen in the name of Adam Goffe in a document dated 1341. It is easy to see how the Tilgate, Heathy Farm, Hillside Inn, Froghsill Farm, and Turners take existing place names. The Flight Tavern clearly refers to its location on the very edge of the area of Gatwick

A reminder this part of Crawley was given over to apple production.

Airport, although the image of the Spitfire on the sign is unlikely to be landing here today.

The Hogshead is an advert for the product, this being a large cask for wine or beer, while the Old Punch Bowl is an advertisement for a drink which it may come as a surprise to find being served in England at least as long ago as 1630. As a pub name, there is no older name in the land than the Grapes, it being known here since Roman times. Clearly this refers to the fruit used to produce the drink.

The Jubilee Oak took its name from the tree which stands outside; this was planted in 1887 by Lord de Blaquiere as part of the Diamond Jubilee celebrations of Queen Victoria. Similarly the Apple Tree would have been used as a marker, as indeed is the Windmill. The Hedgehog Inn is an unusual name, probably derived from the image of the spiny nocturnal insectivorous mammal. The Snooty Fox is an increasingly common name, the image of the fox lending itself well when anthropomorphised as a monocled dandy in top hat and tails.

Downsman is a very unusual name, clearly referring to a person associated with the South Downs, the idea probably occurred to someone when they saw a Dalesman associated with the Dales. Rose and Crown shows this is a patriotic establishment, the rose representing the county and the crown its monarch. On the face of it the White Knight is a chess piece, however, here it specifically refers to the character in Lewis Carroll's *Alice in Wonderland* who is portrayed as an eccentric inventor but ironically a terrible horseman.

The Moonraker is said to be southern England's answer to the stories of the *Wise Men of Gotham*. In this version the men are caught by the excise men when attempting to retrieve contraband casks of brandy from beneath the water. They are allowed to go free when they tell the officers they are pulling the large cheese from the water, that 'cheese' actually the reflection of the moon.

The trade of the Charcoal Burner can be traced back to at least Saxon times. Prior to the use of coal as a fuel, charcoal burners produced as pure a form of carbon as possible in order to smelt ores of metals. This was achieved by gathering wood which would be cut to roughly equal sizes and stacked in a mound. By covering the mound of wood with turf it restricts the oxygen supply and hopefully produces a steady smoulder rather than a fire removing moisture and impurities. The process took a few days but had to be watched continually by the charcoal burner to ensure the fire did not go out nor consume the wood. Obviously a very boring job and thus they took to balancing on a one-legged stool and thus if sleep should overtake them they would be woken when they fell. This is the origin of the phrase 'to drop off' meaning to sleep.

Crawley Down

Recorded as Crauledun in 1272, again this is Old English *crawe leah* with the addition of *dun*. This name describes 'the hill of the woodland clearing frequented by crows'.

While the Royal Oak most certainly refers to the flight of Charles II from the Battle of Worcester in 1651, the Dukes Head is more difficult. A nice caricature of an obviously Georgian gent in profile may not be based on anyone in particular. There are other dukely images but, as the management reported, nobody really knows who this noble gent is.

Cuckfield

Found as Kukefeld and Kukufeld in the late 11th century, this is from Old English *cucu feld* and describes 'the open land where the cuckoo is found'.

Ansty is from *anstig*, an Old English term specifically used to describe a 'narrow or lonely track or one linking two more important routes'. Bulnore describes 'the *ora* or bank of land where bulls are reared'. From Old English *heald leah* comes Hanley or 'the woodland clearing on a slope'. Pilstye Farm is situated on or near 'the *stig* or path of a man called Pila'. Sidney Farm comes from *sud en ea* meaning 'south of the water'. Sugworth Farm speaks of 'the *worth* or enclosure of a man called Sucga'. What began as 'the ford of a man called Wyrtella' is now seen as Wortleford.

Defining almost any name tells something of the history of the place, a glimpse into its past which no scribe would record and no artist paint. Here are two names of very different origins which provide a unique insight into the history of Cuckfield. Henmead is comparatively recent, coming from the early 17th century and telling us this land was rented for the princely sum of one hen and 12 eggs.

The second example is Bentley Farm, a common place name from *beonet leah* 'the woodland clearing where bent grass grows'. Grasses are a comparatively recent development on the evolutionary timescale and, being perfectly adapted to present-day environments, among the most successful. As a group the grasses have developed one very different strategy on which their great success is based. All plants grow from the tip, which is why ivy climbs walls and your garden clematis can be trained up a trellis, but grasses grow from the root base. Hence grazing will not kill or harm the plant, indeed cropping the grass encourages fresh new growth.

Yet no matter how well adapted grasses are, as yet not one has adapted to grow bent as the name of Bentley suggests. Grass has developed to grow quickly and be cropped regularly; if allowed to grow unchecked a breeze or shower of rain will see it collapse under its own weight. Hence we can deduce this area was fenced off, for no wild animals gathered here to graze the grass, nor were livestock penned here, or crops cultivated. However, it was blocked off in some way, and was not waste land. Thus the landholder must have been wealthy enough to allow this to remain untouched for a sufficient length of time in order for the place name to become permanent.

As a pub name the Talbot refers to it being associated with fox hunting, this being the white dog with black ears, the forerunner of today's fox hounds. The Rose and Crown shows this was a patriotic establishment, represented by the rose, and, in the crown, also a royalist supporter. The Wheatsheaf is heraldic, an image used by bodies representing both brewers and bakers.

The Ship Inn would seem an obvious link to the sea, and this may indeed be the origin. However, there is evidence that many inland 'Ships' are actually corruptions of the original *scep* or 'sheep'. Such establishments would have acted as staging posts on trading routes and the Ship Inn at Cuckfield is found at a very obvious road junction.

August Bank Holiday Monday 1965 saw the 15th running of the Donkey Grand National. This annual event raised money for the benefit of good causes in

Cuckfield until a compulsory purchase order took away the venue. However, this did not put an end to fund raising, for it was replaced by the Annual Mayor's Election with votes costing the pre-decimal sixpence (2½ pence). Thus in 1965 Cuckfield, with tongue firmly thrust inside the proverbial cheek, declared itself independent. Every year monies raised here go to Cuckfield, while anything collected by the stallholders at the Cuckoo Fayre is permitted to be given to any charitable cause.

Dean (East & West)

Two places with a common origin of Old English *denu* or 'valley'. The additions, which require no explanation, are first seen in 1150 as Estdena and Westdena respectively, with the earlier record of Dene in the eighth century.

Didling

Records of this name include Dedelinges in the 12th century, Dudelinges in 1230, Didelinge in 1260, and Dedlinge in 1545. Here we find a Saxon personal name with Old English *inga* to tell of the '(place) of the family or followers of a man called Dyddel'.

Donnington

Found as Dunkentone in 966 and as Cloninctune in 1086, this comes from a Saxon personal name and Old English *tun* or 'the farmstead of a man called Dunnuca'.

Duncton

Domesday records this name as Donechitone in 1086; featuring a Saxon personal name and Old English *tun* this is 'the farmstead of a man called Duunuca'.

Locally we find Ridlington Farm, from Old English *ing tun* and a Saxon personal name this is 'the farmstead associated with a man called Wyrtel'.

Durrington

The record of Derentune in 1086 shows this to be from a Saxon personal name and Old English *ing tun* and describing 'the farmstead associated with a man called Deora'.

When it came to naming streets one story stands head and shoulders above all others. It is 17 December 1944 and with victory in sight a Lancaster bomber PB355 takes off from RAF Fulbeck in Lincolnshire. With a full payload of incendiary bombs the crew were bound for Munich when they realised they were having problems reaching any altitude above 1,000 feet.

The crew, fighting to keep the aircraft airborne, were determined to keep from crashing on land, the resultant explosion would have proven devastating, and thus they found themselves limping towards the Sussex coast. The aircraft came down just 100 yards from Worthing pier, a plaque was erected there to mark this extraordinary act of heroism. The seven men on board were killed instantly, only one body has ever been found.

Fifty-three years later developers put forward their proposals for street names, which were dismissed as unsuitable by the council. The mayor, Peter Green, suggested honouring those men who saved so many lives and thus we find several roads named from the events of that day in December 1944.

Flying Officer Edward Essenhigh (Pilot) is commemorated by Essenhigh Drive. Sergeant Harry Varey (Flight Engineer) gave his name to Varey Road. Sergeant Len Bourne (Navigator) is remembered by Bourne Close. Flying Sergeant Fred Rees (Wireless Operator) is seen in Rees Close. Sergeant James Moore (Air Gunner) is recalled by Moore Close. Flight Officer Andrew Thomson (Bomb Aimer) gave us Thomson Close. With Callon Close after Flight Sergeant Gordon

Callon (Air Gunner). Added to this are two names showing these were members of the RAF in Squadron Drive and their base in Fulbeck Avenue.

Minor names here include Munery's Copse, a lasting reminder of former resident John Monte Gomorre (Montgomery), listed as living here in 1332. Salvington puts together a Saxon personal name and Old English *ing tun* and speaks of 'the farmstead associated with a man called Saelaf'. Similarly Offington is 'the farmstead associated with a man called Offa'. Incidentally there is no reason to believe this refers to King Offa, after whom the barrier between England and Wales, Offa's Dyke, was named. Much as the naming of a new royal today sees the name copied for registrations of births for several years, this would also have been true in Saxon times – and Offa ruled for a very long time.

The Lamb Inn shows a link to the church, the lamb representing Jesus Christ, also known as the Lamb of God.

Earnley

Listed as Earneleagh in the eighth century, this comes from Old English *earn leah* and describes 'the woodland clearing where eagles are seen'.

Eartham

A name found as Ercheham in the 12th century and as Ertham in 1279. From Old English *erth ham* this tells of 'the homestead of or by the ploughed land'.

Easebourne

Recorded as Eseburne in *Domesday*, this features a Saxon personal name and Old English *burna* and refers to 'the stream of a man called Esa'.

Buddington features three elements where *inga tun* follow the Saxon personal name and tell us it was 'the farmstead of the family or followers of a man called Budda'. This definition also tells us the man himself was not here, at least not by the time the place was named, but is a reminder of his people or family. Another personal name appears in that of Todham, which comes from 'the *ham* or homestead of a man called Tada'.

Despite Grevatt's appearing to have the possessive, the true origin is Old English *grafan atte* telling us it was 'the place to dig at', a quarry. The name was probably taken by a family at some time in its history, thus the name was misunderstood and given what seems to be a possessive 's'.

As a pub name the White Horse is heraldic and a reference to the royal House of Hanover who reigned in England from 1714 to 1901.

East Dean

From Old English *east denu* comes a name listed as Esdene in *Domesday*. Here the name tells us this place was 'the eastern valley', that is relative to Westdean.

What began as 'the valley of a man called Maegla' is today seen as Malecomb. Selhurst is from *sele ersc* 'the wooded hill with or by a building'. The twin names of Open Winkins and Closed Winkins share the element *wince* meaning 'corner place', the additions are self-explanatory.

Eastergate

Found as Gate in the *Domesday* record of 1086 and as Estergat in 1263, here is a name which was originally simply Old English *geat* 'gate, gap'. Later we find the additional *easterra* or 'further to the east', to distinguish this from Westergate.

Wilkes Head is a local pub named after John Wilkes. A political reformer who fought for the rights of voters, pushed through a bill forcing the publishing of parliamentary debate without editing, and supported the American rebels during the American War of Independence. He is remembered as a man of the people.

East Preston

A name found as Prestetune in 1086 and as Prestona in 1179, this Old English place name is from *preost tun* and speaks of 'the farmstead of the priests'. The addition is to distinguish this from another Preston, that of West Preston in Rustington.

Pubs here include the Roundstone, itself named for Roundstone Lane and almost certainly the last remaining reference to a stone which probably acted as a boundary marker. Despite its name the Tudor Tavern is not from the Tudor age, nor indeed is it painted black and white in the style which is not Tudor but Victorian. Here the reference is the red rose representing the House of Tudor and a refreshing different show of support for the monarchy.

The Clockhouse Bar is easily seen just by looking up to the top of the building on the corner of Sea Road, the large clock face still keeps perfect time. Similarly the Seaview tells of its location almost on the beach itself.

Edburton

Found as Eadburgeton in the 12th century, this name tells of 'the farmstead of a woman called Eadburh' with the Saxon personal name followed by Old English *tun*.

Truleigh Farm derives its name from Old English *treow leah*, describing 'the tree of or by the woodland clearing'. This may seem something of an oxymoron, however, it makes more sense if we realise the tree would have been quite obvious and probably used as a marker.

Egdean

Early listings of this name include Egedene in 1279 and as Eggedon in 1288. Thus here is a Saxon personal name with Old English *denu* to tell of 'the valley of a man called Ecga'.

Locally we find Bleatham, from Old English *bleat hamm* 'the hemmed-in naked or bare place', that is devoid of vegetation. Flexham comes from *fleax hamm* and tells of 'the hemmed-in land where flax grows'.

Elsted

A name found as Halestede in 1086 and as Ellesteda in 1180, this comes from Old English *elle sted* and describes 'the place where elder trees grow'.

Marsh Peak is flatland where the wetland is between two roads, these making the apparent shape of the 'peak' when viewed from above.

Ems, River

Another river in Sussex named from a place, the process known as back-formation. Here the place is 'the enclosure of a man called Aemele', today the village of Emsworth in neighbouring Hampshire.

Felpham

Here is a name from Old English *felh hamm* which describes 'the fallow hemmed-in land'. The name is recorded as Felhhamm in the late ninth century and as Falcheham in *Domesday*.

The George Inn, Felpham.

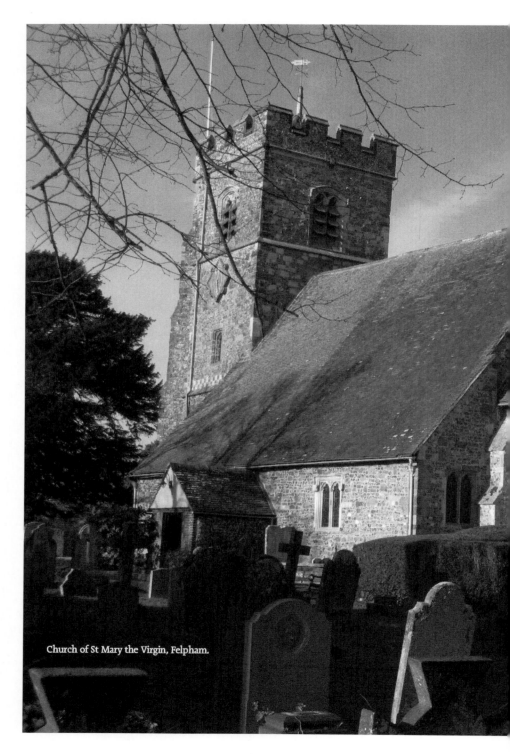

Church of St Mary the Virgin, Felpham.

Ancton speaks of 'the *tun* or farmstead of a man called Anneca'. Flansham tells of 'the *ham* or homestead of a man called Flaem'. While Stanover Lane comes from *stan ora* 'the stony bank of land'.

The Thatched House may seem to speak for itself, yet today only thatching is seen on the image on the sign. The George Inn depicts the very clear image of the patron saint of England, St George. The Fox Inn was probably chosen to represent the image of an animal seen as sly, crafty, and always likeable. Outside the Fox is a plaque telling how poet and painter William Blake was arrested here in 1803 after '...allegedly making seditious remarks billeted at The Fox Inn'. A second plaque here tells of George Morland, an artist who 'Painted a ship leaving Chichester Harbour on a wall of the original Fox Inn in lieu of rent'.

Fernhurst

This name has changed little since the original Old English *fearn hyrst* and still describes 'the wooded hill where ferns grow'.

Henley is a common place name which has several different origins. Here it comes from *hund leah* 'the woodland clearing where hounds are seen', more likely to be where they were reared for a specific purpose rather than a feral population. Verdley shares the suffix, here *fierd leah* speaks of 'the woodland clearing of the army', a pointer to an encampment rather than a battle site.

Telegraph Hill is a much more recent name, a reminder that this was one part of a communication line linking Portsmouth with London during the Napoleonic Wars. Cavalry Quarters recalls 1643, when Royalist cavalry hid here while the opposing Parliamentarian forces were occupying nearby Cowdray.

Ferring

The earliest record of this name dates from 765 and is exactly as it appears today, although by the *Domesday* record of 1086 this had become Feringes.

Here is a Saxon personal name and Old English *inga* telling of the '(place of) the family or followers of a man called Fera'.

The Tudor Close is a pub which probably took the name of a smallholding or field associated with a man with the family name Tudor. It certainly was not because the building dates from that era, these buildings were built in the middle of the 18th century. Before World War One it was home to songwriter Paul Rubens, while between the wars it served as Tudor Close Preparatory School for Boys. The Henty Arms recalls the family who did much for the village, while also advertising the brewers of Henty and Constable.

Findon

Listed as Findune in the *Domesday* record of 1086 and coming from Old English *fin dun*, this name refers to 'the hill with a heap of wood on it'.

Locally we find Mundham Court, a recent home which gets its name from a Saxon one for this was 'the homestead of a man called Munda'. Nepcote

Steep Lane, Findon.

Eleventh century church of
St John the Baptist, Findon.

features two elements, *nep* and *cote*. The former is a dialect word for 'catmint', the suffix means 'cottage' but the only similarity with the modern idea would be the thatched roof, for this would be a hovel or shed and probably shared with the animals. Ramsdean is from Old English *hraefn dun* 'the hill frequented by ravens'.

The Black Horse public house undoubtedly gets its name from a coat of arms. However, this heraldic image is so common it is extremely difficult to know where the name originated. First mentioned in 1701, the Gun Inn was not only an inn but a gunsmith's shop too.

Fishbourne

Listed as Fiseborne in the *Domesday* record of 1086, this is derived from Old English *fisc burna* and, not surprisingly, refers to 'the stream where fish are caught'.

East Broyle and West Broyle share a common element telling us there was an enclosed park here, well stocked with deer and other animals of the chase. Saltmill is easily seen as referring to the former salt works here.

Fittleworth

Seen as Fitelwurtha in 1168, this comes from a Saxon personal name with the addition of Old English *worth* giving 'the enclosure of a man called Fitela'.

Minor place names of this parish include Bedham, the '*ham* or homestead of a man called Buda'. Little Bognor is a transferred name from the resort of Bognor Regis, why it was chosen will never be known. Hesworth Common began life as a settlement known as 'the *worth* or enclosure of a man called Here'. Limbourne Farm is either *lin burna* 'the stream near where flax grows' or *lind burna* 'the stream near the lime trees'. Lithersgate Common is from *hlip gaet* or 'the gate or way on the slope'. Lastly Sond is from a word which is the same today as it was in Saxon times, *sand* describing the soil.

Flansham

A name listed as Flennesham in 1220, here an uncertain first element (probably a personal name) precedes either Old English *ham* 'homestead' or *hamm* 'hemmed-in area'. Without further records, preferably prior to the 13th century, this name will probably never be fully understood.

Fletching

Found as Flecinges in *Domesday*, this is derived from a Saxon personal name and Old English *inga* to refer to the '(place of) the family or followers of a man called Flecci'.

Ford

An element often seen as a suffix in a place name but also a common enough name in its own right. This name is found as Fordes at the end of the 12th century, showing that what is today *ford* or 'river crossing' was originally plural.

Pub names include the Ship and Anchor, clearly a maritime reference and probably referring to the former career of a landlord.

Fulking

Records of this name include Fochings in *Domesday* and Folkinges at the end of the 11th century. The name describes the '(place of) the family or followers of a man called Folca', where the Saxon personal name is followed by Old English *ings*.

Clapper is a very specific term and describes 'a plank of wood laid across a stream as a footbridge'. Paythorne Barn was built near 'the thorn bush of a man called Paga'. Perching Farm was land once associated with 'the people of the enclosure'.

Today we often find street names in the middle of the largest city which suggest a rural location. Modern developers are convinced naming the road on the new estate The Meadows attracts much more interest than New Street. Traditionally the same was also true of public houses where a rural scene, such as the image from the local name of the Shepherd and Dog, suggest a more peaceful location. In the case of the Shepherd and Dog at Fulking this remains the case.

Funtington

Listed as Fundintune in the 12th century, this is from Old English *funta ing tun* and speaks of this as 'the farmstead associated with the spring'.

Local names include East Ashling and West Ashling, which share an origin from a Saxon personal name with Old English *inga tun* or 'the farmstead of the family or followers of a man called Aescel'. Chalcroft Copse is named for 'the smallholding where calves are reared'; Densworth speaks of the *worth* or enclosure of a man called Dene'; and Ratham has the suffix *ham* telling of 'the homestead of a man called Rota'.

Goring by Sea

Found as Garinges in the *Domesday* record of 1086, this name features a Saxon personal name and Old English *inga* telling of the '(place of) the family or followers of a man called Gara'. The addition is very recent and requires no explanation.

Knell House comes from Old English *cnoll*, initially meaning 'hilltop' but later also used to describe 'hillock'.

The Golden Lion, as with nearly every pub name featuring an oddly coloured animal, is heraldic. A popular image, it has been used by many families, most notably Henry I and the Percy family, dukes of Northumberland. Origins of the Sussex Yeoman depends upon the use of 'yeoman', either this is a soldier, a farmer, or trusted servant. The Mulberry must be an heraldic device, although just who or what it represents is uncertain. What may prove surprising is this has been known in heraldry since the reign of Henry III. However, the best name here is the Swallow's Return, a suggestion that this refers to the very epitome of a migratory bird. However, it could also be seen as an invitation to drink at these premises again.

Graffham

Domesday's record of Grafham in 1086 points to an origin of Old English *graf ham* and 'the homestead by a grove'.

Tegleaze comes from *teg laes* 'the pasture where yearling sheep are grazed', letting us see this was where sheep were reared. Woodcote farm began life as *wudu cot* 'the cottage by or in the wood'.

Pubs include the White Horse, an heraldic image representing the House of Hanover, and the Foresters Arms, showing this was a meeting place or court of the friendly society known as the Ancient Order of Foresters.

Greatham

A name easily seen as coming from Old English *great ham* or 'the great homestead', the only query is just how this was seen as 'great'. If this, as seems likely, is a reference to size, it must be a late Saxon name and an example of the early use of *great*, for normally 'great' would be represented by *micel*. The surviving forms of Gretham in 1086, Greteham in 1121, Gretham in 1230, Gratham in 1510, and Gritham in 1724 are too late to show when the place was first settled or named.

Locally we find Washingham, from Old English *waesse inga hamm* 'the people of the hemmed-in wet place'.

Grinstead, East

A name meaning quite literally 'the green place', understood to refer to 'the pasture for grazing'. This name, recorded as Grenesteda in 1121, comes from Old English *grene stede*.

Here is Botley Wood, the woodland taking the name of a nearby area which began as 'the *leah* or woodland clearing of a man called Botta'. Fairlight Farm is derived from Old English *fearn leah*, which speaks of 'the woodland clearing where ferns grow'. From a Saxon personal name and Old English *denn* comes Hackenden, a name describing 'the swine pasture of a man called Hacca'.

Hairley Farm is from *ora leah*, a name referring to 'the sloping woodland clearing'. Saint Hill has no religious connection, this remembers a fire as 'the singed or burned hill'. With a name describing 'the corner of land where raspberries grow', the name was then passed to the building of Imberhorne Manor. Shovelstrode Farm is derived from *scylf strod*, Old English for 'the marshy ground by a slope'. Tilkhurst is another Old English name, here referring to 'the wooded hill of young oaks'.

As a pub name the Star began as a religious image. The most obvious link is to the star of Bethlehem, although most often this represents the Virgin Mary. The Prince of Wales does not show an image of any particular holder of the title, yet the vast majority refer to the future Edward VII who, until 20 April 2011, had held the title for longer than anyone, 59 years two months and 13 days. Another royal name is that of the Rose and Crown, here the landlord showed his establishment was that of a royalist (in the crown) and a patriot (represented by the rose). That link to the monarchy is also seen in the Crown.

Certainly heraldic, the White Lion is probably representative of the dukes of Norfolk, their seat at nearby Arundel. However, this powerful image was also used by the earls of March, and Edward IV. The Ship does not seem to refer to a specific vessel, hence likely a link to an old mariner. While this particular building is not old enough, it may have replaced a similarly named pub from a much earlier age and, in the case of the earlier example, most often a corruption of Old English *scep* of 'sheep' representing the wool trade.

Gamebird is a name which began as an alternative to Gamecock, the breed used in cock fights, although today it is used to refer to those breeds suitable for hunting, and particularly the table. The Ounce and Ivy Bush almost sounds as if it was born to be a pub name, it is derived from the coat of arms of the Sackville

Prince of Wales public house in East Grinstead.

family who were great landowners in the region. The family were also dukes of Dorset, the same coat of arms spoken of in the Dorset Arms. Similarly named is the Sussex Arms.

It would have been a great disappointment to find the Guinea Pig was named for a favourite pet. Thankfully the real origin features the other use of the term, an examination, a revealing insight into history so modern it could be argued, especially in the context of place names, it hardly qualifies as history at all. During World War Two the nearby hospital saw the arrival of Sir Archibald McIndoe and his colleagues and the founding of a highly specialised plastic surgery unit. The 600 patients, nearly all injured in incidents involving aircraft, instantly became members of the Guinea Pig Club. The sign is worthy of mention too, for it features a winged guinea pig in a headlong dive and on fire, with a battle-scarred Spitfire behind.

More obvious are those names showing the earlier uses for the Coach House and the Old Mill. The Intrepid Fox, however, is not simply another reference to the ubiquitous vulpine, this Fox is a surname. Charles James Fox was an 18th century statesman who was very vocal in speaking out against the British policies during the American War and also campaigned for the abolition of the slave trade and political freedom for dissenters.

Grinstead, West

A second name describing 'the pasture used for grazing' from Old English *grene stede*. The addition is to distinguish this from the previous entry and is seen as early as the record of Westgrenested in 1280.

Bassell's Farm comes from *syle* which follows a Saxon personal name to speak of 'the wallowing place of a man called Baedda'. Of course this is not suggesting the man himself wallowed here, simply wallowing occurred and Baedda held the land. Hatterell is from the Old French *haterel*, pointing to the 'apex, the crown of the hill'. Honey Bridge is a common name which never refers to the natural produce but to 'muddy, sticky land'. Posbrook's Farm is from *pise broc* 'the brook near where peas are grown'. Lastly Whitenwick Barn is a reminder of 'the *wic* or specialised farm of a man called Hwita'. Almost every *wic* would have specialised in dairy produce.

Halnaker

Recorded as Helnache in the *Domesday* record of 1086. This name is from Old English *healf aecer* and describes this area as 'half an acre'.

The local is the Anglesey Arms, named after the Marquis of Anglesey. General Henry William Paget (1768–1854) commanded the British cavalry at Waterloo in 1815. During the battle he lost a leg and, which could never happen today, that limb was kept for 40 years until he died and all were reunited in burial.

Handcross

This is a name without a surviving record dating from before 1617 where it appears as Handcrosse. Perhaps this is quite late and refers to 'a junction where five roads meet', with the signpost thus resembling a hand.

The Fountain Inn has two equally likely origins. Most obvious is the reference to a local spring, however, statistically speaking this is the least likely as a reliable source of water is a must for any pub. More common is the alternative heraldic image, one used by both the Plumbers' Company and the Master Mariners.

The Red Lion most often shows a link to Scotland, either through ownership of the land or an early landlord, this being the most common pub name in England. Second on that list is a pub name also found here, the Royal Oak remembering the flight of Charles II from the Battle of Worcester in 1651 and when he hid in the branches of a huge oak tree to avoid capture by the Parliamentarians.

Hangleton

Listed as Hangetone in 1086, as Hangeltune in 1091, and as Hengelton in 1248, this is from Old English *hangra tun* and literally describes 'the farmstead by the overhanging wood'. Here 'overhanging' refers to the woodland being above the settlement, perhaps appearing to overhang it from certain angles.

Hardham

Old English *ham* follows a Saxon personal name and describes 'the hemmed-in land of a woman called Heregyth'. The earliest record is as Heriedeham in the *Domesday* survey of 1086.

Harting (East & South)

Found as Hertingas in 970 and as Hertinges in 1086, these places have a common origin, hence the self-explanatory additions. Derived from a Saxon personal name and Old English *inga* this place began as the '(place of) the family or followers of a man called Heort'.

Bridger's Pond recalls 1350, when one Domenic Brugg is recalled as being here. Eckenfields is from *feld* 'the open land of a man called Eccen'. Harehurst Wood has nothing to do with our native lagomorph, here the name describes 'the boundary wood'. Main Down began life as 'the *dun* or hill associated with a man called Maega'. Nyewood represents Old English *niwe wudu* 'the new wood', not seen as being newly planted but more recently utilised. Poppets is from *puca pytt*, a warning this was 'the pit haunted by a goblin'.

Hassocks

This is a very recent settlement which was laid out in the 19th century. However, the name is much older, a field name coming from Old English *hassuc* and describing 'the clumps of coarse grass'.

Pubs named the Sportsman were named to show many games and sports were played or organised within. This was originally two pubs, the Magpie and the Sportsman, before being knocked into one. There is no doubting when customers have found the Thatched Inn, the name tells us exactly what to look for, and visitors looking for the Hassocks Hotel know exactly where to go. Friars Oak also uses its name to tell visitors to look out for an oak tree which marks the premises, while also referring to the land being owned by the church.

The Duke of York Inn takes the name of the eponymous character in the nursery rhyme *The Grand Old Duke of York*. Although there have been many to hold this title, it is traditionally given to the second son of the reigning monarch on the occasion of his marriage, the one in question here is Frederick Augustus (1763–1827). Son of George III, he commanded the English forces in Flanders. However, the rhyme leaves us with a false impression of this man. Firstly he did not have 10,000 men, at least 30,000 were under his command. They were not marched up nor down hills, for this county is very flat indeed, and while he may well have been grand, he was in no way old, having reached his 32nd birthday shortly before the conflict ended.

Haywards Heath

Documented as Heyworth in 1261 and as Haywards Hoth in 1544, this shows an Old English origin of *hege worth* or 'the enclosure with a hedge'. It is not until much later that we see the addition of *haeth* or 'heath'.

Boltro Road is derived from *bula trag* or 'the trough where bulls are watered'. Scrace Bridge recalls 1544, when the family of John Skrak were living here.

Pubs include the Burrell Arms, the family who lived at Knepp Castle, actually a John Nash designed castellated mansion built in 1812. The house burned down in 1904 and, although rebuilt, is not open to the public. The Dolphin shows a link to the sea, this mammal seen as the friend and a good omen for sailors. However, this pub has recently been renamed the Sergison Arms, the family included two members of parliament and have been highly influential in the county. The Red Lion is an heraldic image showing a link with Scotland. Another heraldic symbol gave a name to the Star, which symbolises the Virgin Mary. The Golden Eagle is another heraldic image and such a popular one it is difficult to know what or who it represented.

The Heath is self-explanatory, as is the Fox and Hounds seen to symbolise the hunt. The Ansty Cross Inn takes the name of its location, similarly the Pear Tree would have been a marker for this pub. A stop on the coaching route is indicated by the Coach and Horses, a transport link is also seen in the name of the Sloop, possibly an indication this was run by an old sailor. An invitation to those working in the agricultural community is seen at the Farmers Inn.

The Jolly Tanners offers a welcome to locals today, much as it did when named. Workers in the production of leather, a tough job and one considered a most noxious process, found themselves working as far away from the main settlement as possible. It is no wonder the aroma was quite overpowering, for the untreated hide, having been cleaned of hair, was softened by immersion in a mix of water, human urine, animal dung, and rotting flesh. The process was intended to soften the material, which also required workers to knead it by removing their footwear and trampling repeatedly on the raw hide as it was soaking, a process which would take two or three hours. Clearly these workers would have little reason to smile and yet managed to be quite jolly when enjoying the hospitality offered by the Jolly Tanners.

Henfield

Found in 770 as Hanefeld and in 1086 as Hamfelde, this is from Old English *han feld* and speaks of 'the open land characterised by stones or rocks'.

Here we find minor names including Buckwish Farm, marked out as 'the meadow with the beech tree or trees'. Catslands Farm has no connection with felines, here is 'the agricultural land associated with a man called Catt'. Oreham is from *ora hamm* 'the bank or shelf of the hemmed-in land'. Shiprods Farm comes from *rod sceap* 'the clearing where sheep are raised'. Lastly Wantley Farm is a reminder of the settlement known as 'the *leah* or woodland clearing of a man called Wanta'.

One pub name origin we are quite certain of is the Cat and Canary. It was the winner of a competition in 1976, thought to be based on the Warner Brothers cartoon characters Sylvester and Tweety Pie. The Bull Inn may be heraldic or may be as simple as a prized animal.

The Royal Oak recalls the flight of Charles II who hid in an oak tree. Yet the George Inn is named, not from a king but, from the patron saint of England, St George. The Gardeners Arms probably offers hospitality to those who worked the land, as does the Plough Inn. Once the generic name for any pub the White Hart retains its popularity, as does the Fox which would have started as an easily recognised image.

Heyshott

Appearing as Hathsete at the end of the 11th century, this is an Old English place name from *haeth sceat* and describes 'the corner of land where heather grows'.

Hoathly, West

Another 'woodland clearing where heather grows', the addition distinguishes this from the previous entry. This example is listed as Hadlega in 1121.

Chiddingly Wood derives its name from a Saxon personal name and Old English *inga leah* telling of 'the woodland clearing of the family or followers of a man called Citta'. Meaning 'the swine pasture of a man called Hemele' it comes from the name Hammingden. Pickeridge was once 'the ridge of land where pigs are reared'. Tickeridge is from *teag hrycg* or 'the ridge of land with a tye'. A tye referred to 'common land'.

Local pubs include the Cat Inn, most likely named after a favourite pet, and the White Hart Inn, later a generic term for all pubs after it first came to prominence as the symbol for Richard II.

Horsham

The earliest surviving record of this name dates from 947 where it appears exactly as it does today. Indeed the original Old English is exactly the same, *hors ham* referring to 'the homestead where horses are kept'.

The street names of Horsham tell their own history of the place. Agate Lane was named after the family who were successful as both farmers and corn merchants from the 16th century. Albery Close remembers William Albery, a saddler who also helped set up the local museum. Boyce Close remembers David Boyce, owner of a furniture store here. Chart Way features the surname of the man who was a merchant dealing in corn and coal.

Copnall Way is named after a Mr Copnall, whose photographic studio was here for many years. Mr Collett's baker shop was at what is now known as Collett's Alley. Moons Lane recalls Thomas Moon, a tanner and leather merchant. Parson's Walk and Stan's Way remember Stan Parsons, said to have done more than anyone to ensure the prosperity of the town during the 20th century.

Barttelot Road recalls Sir Walter Barttelot, who was a member of parliament for Horsham from 1887 to 1893. Bostock Avenue is after Dr Edward Bostock, a governor of Collyer's School, the Chairman of the Union Workhouse Hospital Board, and Justice of the Peace. He fathered 11 children, although three of his sons were killed in World War One. Eyles Close recalls Albert Hope Eyles, who served the community as a councillor and oversaw their eduction as headmaster of the Victory Boys School in the 1930s.

George Pinion Court remembers the man who was the proprietor of two hairdressing salons in Horsham. Lieutenant Colonel J. Innes bought the Roffey Park estate in the 1880s, this land is now where Innes Road is situated. Mr Naldrett did much work for the elderly and local charities, deserving the naming of Naldrett Close.

Thomas Oliver, who earned his money as a railway engineer in the Victorian era, built Tanbridge House which is where Oliver Road is now found. Redford Avenue was named by the developer, a Mr Redford. Padwick Road remembers Mr Padwick, a lawyer, moneylender and habitual gambler. Vernon Close recalls Colonel Vernon, a World War One veteran and man of the parish who served as church warden.

Among those names of unique origin is Ben's Close, cut near the fields where a horse called Ben was pastured. Depot Road is where a large armory depot was located during the Napoleonic Wars. The Dog and Bacon public house has no true etymology, it is a corruption of 'Dorking Beacon'.

Local names include Benhams, from *bean hamm* or 'the hemmed-in land where beans are grown'. Bishopric Farm is a reminder of the fairs held here, chartered by the Archbishop of Canterbury. Carfax is one of the most common English place names from Old French, this describing 'where four roads meet'. Chesworth Farm began as 'the *worth* or enclosure of a man called Ceorra'. Roffey comes from *ruh geheag* 'the rough clearing', that is one with uneven land. Early forms of Tanbridge suggest there was a tannery here, the name later associated with the bridge.

Sluts Cottages was not a place of ill-repute, here the name comes from Old English *sliete* meaning 'mud'. However, that this is Sluts and not Slut could well point to *sliete* being used as a nickname, the final 's' would therefore be possessive.

The original use of the Black Swan as a pub name was used to refer to something very rare, for at the time it was thought every swan in the world was white. When Captain James Cook discovered the black swan to be native to Australia the term came to be used to refer to anything Australian. In either case locals would often humorously refer to it as the dirty duck or, as the case here, the Mucky Duck.

The Fox Inn is as common a name as the mammal, the most likely reason for this choice of name. The Partridge hangs a sign featuring an image of the bird, however, this is taken from the name of Partridge Green, itself a family surname. Yet the Coot is a name derived from the common waterbird. Representing the earls of Pembroke comes the Green Dragon. The sign outside the Hornbrook shows a man on a horse blowing a horn, an interesting depiction of a name which is simply a place name describing the shape of the nearby stream.

The Crown aimed to show support for the monarchy and thus the country, as does the Kings Arms. Ye Olde Stout House is indeed somewhere stout was served, although the addition of 'Ye Olde' suggests it is much older than the building appears to be. The Black Jug advertises the product, or rather the container from which ale was served. This is also true of the Malt Shovel, a tool used by brewers. To some degree the Merry Monk also refers to the product, the suggestion of a warm welcome to all, the mention of the religious figure probably taken from an earlier name.

The Bear, featuring a model of a bear above the sign, is probably taken from a relevant coat of arms. A clear reference to the coaching era, and indeed earlier, is found in the name of the Horse and Groom. More contemporary transport

The Dog and Bacon, Horsham.

methods are seen in the Station. The Lynd Cross is named after its location, at a junction between the Bishopric and Springfield Road.

No individual has more pubs named after him than arguably our greatest naval hero, Admiral Lord Horatio Nelson, here given as simply the Nelson. The Shelley Arms recalls the family whose residence at Castle Goring was home to several generations, including the Romantic poet Percy Bysshe Shelley. The

Chequers Inn is an early sign, a reminder of how early inn-keepers would double as moneyers, although the original use indicated a board game similar to draughts was played within.

The Dog and Duck shows the familiar image of the duck hunter and his dog, although there are no ponds which could be associated with this sport nearby today. The Owl, formerly the Wise Old Owl, uses an image to attract visitors, one easily recognised and also associated with the hours of darkness, when most visit the pub. Most likely the Fountain represents a link to the Plumbers' Company or the Master Mariners, a local spring is also a possibility.

The Star is probably an indication this land was owned by the church, the image symbolic of the Virgin Mary, clearly derived from the story of the Star of Bethlehem and often depicted as such. The Cherry Tree Inn is probably named from a nearby tree, although it is also used in heraldry where it is referred to by the French *griotte*. The Holmbush takes an old place name meaning 'the bush by the holm oaks', which hardly fits with the topography and hence is a transferred name. The Sussex Barn is a new building, one designed to resemble a refurbished barn.

A patriotic name is seen in the George and Dragon, a reference to the patron saint of England and his most famous deed, the slaying of the dragon. An heraldic image is seen at the Rising Sun, an image representing many families, and former Kings Edward III and Richard III. Whilst, as the saying goes, 'an Englishman's home is his castle', the Bax Castle public house could hardly be described as a 'castle'. Here is a 15th-century building and former home to a weaver by the name of Bax, hence the name.

The Queens Head displays a very obvious image of Queen Elizabeth I, however, this is not the origin of a pub clearly constructed centuries after the line of the royal House of Tudor was extinct. The name was probably taken from the road on which it stands, Queens Street. Another name referring to the location is the Tanners Arms, although this reference dates from many years ago. The Bedford shows an image which comes from the dukes of Bedford, important landholders since the 17th century.

A friendly society with lodges or courts in both the United States and the United Kingdom, the Ancient Order of Foresters would meet at the Foresters Arms. The Dun Horse Inn most likely recalls a favourite animal, here 'dun' refers to a brownish-grey colouring. The White Horse is quite different, this being heraldic and symbolises the House of Hanover. Similarly the Wheatsheaf is a device used in the arms of both the Worshipful Company of Bakers and also the Brewers' Company.

The Boar's Head can be traced to the 14th century, when the head served with an apple in its mouth made for an impressive sight at the Christmas feast. The Windmill is a common pub name, one noting the nearby smock windmill which is still in full working order. At the Green Man the reference is to the forester or woodsman, once a very important member of the community.

The Crown Inn is a very obvious show of patriotism by way of support for the monarchy. Baron Selsey was a title created for Sir James Peachey in the late 18th century, the titles and line died out along with the third baron in 1838. However, the crest lives on outside the Selsey Arms. Several sources have been attributed to the use of Hen and Chickens as a pub name, including a children's game similar to tiddlywinks. The most likely is religious, in Christian symbolism the hen with chickens is a representation of God's providence.

Horsted Keynes

Found as simply Horstede in 1086, this is derived from Old English *hors stede* and 'the place where horses are kept'. In 1307 we find Horsted Kaynes, the addition showing possession by the family beginning with William de Cahaignes by 1086.

Local names begin with Belvedere, a fairly common name from the Old French for 'beautiful view'. Leamland is Old English, a name referring to 'the fallow enclosure'. Vox End comes from Old English *feax*, literally 'hair' but surely refers to vegetation.

The Crown Inn shows a link to the monarchy, possibly as a patriot or equally likely is this being on land owned by the King. The Green Man is derived from the sign, this image originally intended to represent the woodsman, a very important member of the community in earlier times.

Houghton

A common place name and one normally found with a second defining element. Here Old English *hoh tun* tells of 'the farmstead at the spur of land'. The name appears as Hohtun in a document dated 683.

Wapelgate Corner is a minor place name which points to an origin of *wapple gaet*, two words which describe the same feature. Old English *gaet* refers to 'the way', while *wapple* is a dialect term for a bridal path.

Hunston

Listed as Hunestan in the *Domesday* survey of 1086, this features Old English *stan* and a Saxon personal name giving 'the boundary stone of a man called Huna'.

Kipson Bank is derived from 'the *tun* or farmstead of a man called Cyppi'.

Hurstpierpoint

Domesday lists this as simply Herst, derived from Old English *hyrst* this is 'the wooded hill'. Normally this element is seen as a suffix and thus it is no surprise to find the addition in a document of 1279 as Herst Perepunt, itself referring to possession by one Robert de Pierpoint by the time of *Domesday*.

Hunston village sign.

Goldbridge House was built on land previously known for growing a golden or yellow flower. The oddly-named Danny is a minor place name derived from *denu eg* 'the dry land by the marsh in a valley'.

Pub names here begin with the White Horse, most often heraldic and a reference to the House of Hanover, whose six monarchs – George I, George II, George III, George IV, William IV, Victoria – reigned from 1714 until 1901. It is not clear how the Poacher became a pub name. Perhaps as the old saying goes 'the poacher makes the best gamekeeper', he would also become a decent landlord with game often on the menu. However, we should not entirely rule out the folksong of the *Lincolnshire Poacher*.

The New Inn is one of the most common of pub names, the name telling us there was already a pub here when this was built. However, it could never be seen as 'new' today for it dates from the middle of the 15th century. Hence a better name might be Newer Inn.

I

Ifield

Found as Ifelt in 1086, the *Domesday* record shows this to be from Old English *ig feld* and speaks of 'the open land where yew trees grow'.

Local names include Stafford House, built near the *steor ford* 'the ford used by steers or cattle'. Stumbleholm Farm is a term of contempt, referring to 'the *holmr* or raised ground in a marsh one may stumble upon', suggesting it was unremarkable or insignificant.

The Plough is an early pub name, offering hospitality to a workforce which invariably earned a living off the land. The Gate is an old place name from Old English *geat* which referred to the way and not to any barrier across it. Charles II's hiding place in the Boscobel Oak near Shifnal in Shropshire is commemorated by the Royal Oak.

Ifold

This Old English place name tells of 'the fold in well-watered land' and is derived from *ieg fald*. The earliest surviving record dates from 1296 where it appears exactly as it does today.

Iping

Found as Epingfes in the *Domesday* record of 1086, this is a Saxon personal name and Old English *inga* telling of the '(place of) the family or followers of a man called Ipa'.

Locally we find Fitzhall, a personal name followed by *halh* and telling of 'the nook of land of a man called Fit'. Wardley has a different suffix *leah* giving us 'the woodland clearing of a man called Wearda'.

Iridge

This Old English place name tells of 'the ridge of land where yew trees grow'. The name comes from Old English *ig hrycg* and is recorded as Yrugge in 1248 and as Iwrugge.

Itchenor (East & West)

Two places, where the additions are self-explanatory, with a common origin. Recorded as Iccannore in 683 and as Icenore in 1086, here is a Saxon personal name and Old English *ora* giving 'the shore of a man called Icca'.

Itchingfield

Found as Ecchingefeld in 1222, Hecchingefeld in 1225, Herchingfeld in 1230, and Eachyngfeild in 1483. Here is a Saxon personal name with Old English *inga feld* giving 'the open land of the family or followers of a man called Ecci or Hecci'.

Note this is *feld* and not 'field' (or even 'feild' as given in the late 15th-century record). The Saxon *feld* was not the same as the modern field. No neatly clipped hedge or fence, no lockable gate to pen the livestock, this was simply an area which had been manually cleared, with all the brushwood and vegetation pushed back to form an unintentional boundary. Although doubtless both *feld* and field were put to the same uses.

Local names begin with Fulford's Farm, a common minor place name describing 'the foul or muddy ford'. Marlands comes from *maere land* and describes 'the boundary lands'. What began as 'the steep wooded hill' is now seen as Sharpenhurst Farm. Slaughterford is not as gruesome as it sounds, this is derived from *slah treow* Old English for 'the sloe tree'. Possessionhouse Farm was once a part of a larger estate, this part sold off in 1707 but was later recovered and that is exactly what the name describes.

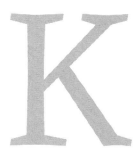

Keymer

A name found as Chemere in 1086, as Kiemera in 1090, and as Keymer for the first time in 1598. There is some slight doubt as to the origin of the first part of this name, however, almost every source will give this as from Old English *cu mere* or 'the pool near where cows are reared'.

Locally the name of Hassocks comes from Old English *hassuc* or the '(place) of rough tussocks of grass'. The Greyhound public house would likely represent an image associated with a major landholder, the dukes of Newcastle.

Kingston by Sea

Recorded as Chingestune in the *Domesday* survey of 1086, as Kyngeston Bouci in 1315, and as Kingeston Bouscy in 1317. Here is Old English *cyninges tun* literally 'the farmstead of the king' and simply a royal manor. The modern addition, distinguishing this from the following example, is self-explanatory but is not quite what it appears. As can be seen from the 14th century examples 'by Sea', while geographically correct, is actually a manorial name, the lord of the manor being the de Bouci or de Boucey family, the surname later Anglicised as Bowsey.

Kirdford

Among the many records of this place name are Kinredeford in 1228, Kenredeford in 1240, Kerredeford in 1248, and as Kerdesforth in 1374. The suffix is clearly Old English *ford*, here following a female Saxon personal name to speak of 'the ford of a woman called Cynethryth'.

Local names here include Barkfold, which describes 'the fold or pen of a man called Beadeca'. What was 'the fold or pen of Ceol' is now marked on the map as Chilsfold, similarly Crawfold is 'the pen or fold where crows are seen'. Frithfold Farm is from *fyrhth falod* 'the pen or fold of or near the sparsely wooded area'. Linfold Farm may either be *lin falod* 'the fold by where flax is grown' or *lind falod* 'the fold by the lime trees'.

Bittlesham describes itself as 'the *ham* or homestead of a man called Betel'. Ebernoe describes itself as being at 'the spur of land by the marshland stream'. Hardnip's Barn could either be describing 'the hard crest of land' or may have been brought here as a family name, Richard de Hardekneppe being listed here in 1239.

From *heafoc hyrst* comes Hawkhurst Court or 'the wooded hill frequented by hawks'. Plaistow is from *pleg stow* 'the assembly place for sports or play'. Scratchings Farm is from the dialect word *cratchings* telling of 'the refuse created by melting down pig fat'. Shillinglee Park represents *scylf ing leah* or 'the woodland clearing associated with the shelf of land'.

The first element of Slifehurst is *slyf* meaning 'sleeve' but used here in a topographical sense to mean 'the wooded hill by the hollow of land'. Sparrwood from *spaer wudu* tells of 'the enclosed wood'. Strudgwick Wood is from *strod wic* or 'the specialised (probably dairy) farm in a marshy place'. Swear Farm is from *sweora* 'the neck of land'. Todhurst is from *tod hyrst* 'the wooded hill of the pollarded trees'. Lastly Wephurst tells us of 'the wooded hill of a man called Waeppa'.

Lancing

Recorded as Lancinges in the *Domesday* survey of 1086, this is a Saxon personal name and Old English *inga* telling of the '(place of) the family or followers of a man called Wlanc'.

Street names of note include Boundstone Lane, a reminder of the times when the parish boundaries were marked by stones. Alma Street was named after the first battle of the Crimean War. A combined force of British, French and Ottoman forces defeated the 33,000 Russian troops in September 1854, who were outnumbered by almost two to one. Caper's Lane took the name of Caper's Field. While Crabtree Lane ran along an area known for its crab apples.

The term *pad* was used to refer to a 'smuggler' or to a place where such nefarious characters would gather. Hence the name of Pad Farm seems rather an unusual origin until we realise the farm took the name of the Pad Inn which once stood here.

The Farmers public house offers refreshment to what can hardly be considered a rural location. Another trade was the inspiration for the Sussex

Church of St James the Less, Lancing.

Potter, and a third by the Three Horseshoes, a name which should be seen as a question and offering the services of a blacksmith.

The Merry Monk can hardly be said to refer to a trade, indeed the relevant part of this name is the first word suggesting a good time can be found within. While the image outside the Crabtree Inn depicts crabs crawling over a large trunk washed up on the shore, the real origin reference is to the crab apple tree outside which served as a marker.

Langney

Listed as Langelie in 1086 and as Langania in 1121, this is from Old English *lang eg* and describes 'the long piece of dry ground in a marsh'.

Lavant (East Lavant)

Two places with a common origin which is seen in the *Domesday* record of Loventone. Here Old English *tun* follows the Celtic river name meaning 'the gliding one' and telling of 'the farmstead on the River Lavant'. By 1227 the name is recorded simply as Lavent, later the second settlement added the self-explanatory 'east'. Raughmere Farm stands by 'the pool frequented by herons', from Old English *hraga mere*.

Pubs here include the Royal Oak, one of the most common pub names in the land, a reminder of Charles II's escape following defeat at the Battle of Worcester. The Earl of March is a title held by the dukes of Richmond, whose family seat is at Goodwood House near Chichester.

Limden, River

Previously this river was known as the Lymbourne. Old English *lim* or 'lime trees' was later suffixed by *denu* or 'valley', thus describing the country through which the Lymbourne flowed before joining the Rother.

Linch

A name listed in the *Domesday* book of 1086 as Lince and as Linche and Lynche in the first half of the 13th century. The name comes from Old English *hlinc* describing 'a hill ridge'.

Minor names here include Den Wood, which comes from *denu* or 'valley'. Hollycombe is from *hol cumb* 'the hollow valley'.

Linchmere

Here a Saxon personal name and Old English *mere* combine to tell us this was 'the pool of a man called Wlenca'. The name is recorded as Wlenchemere in 1161.

Shulbrede Priory took its name from the existing place name. From *scylf braedu* it speaks of 'the broad shelf of land'.

Lindfield

The earliest surviving record of this name comes from the latter half of the eighth century, where it is shown as Lindefeldia. Here Old English *linden feld* speaks of 'the open land where lime trees grow'.

Local names include Buxshalls, which describes 'the buildings by the beech trees'. A Saxon personal name with the suffix *hus*, Cockhaise Farm speaks of 'the house of a man called Cocca'. Walstede Farm similarly features a personal name, here suffixed by *stede* to tell of 'the place of a man called Walca'.

Early records of The Neale can be traced to the Middle English *atten ellern*, meaning 'at the elder tree'. The migration of the final 'n' in *atten* to the beginning of the next word when it starts with a vowel is not just common but to be expected. Indeed, as if to prove such, the name of Noven Farm comes from *atten ofen* or 'at the oven or furnace'.

While the true origin of the Witch public house is unknown, there is a local story as to where this name came from. Handed down from generation to generation, it is said the place was once owned and run by two sisters. As was commonplace at the time they brewed their own ale, rated by their customers as a real 'witch's brew'.

Other names include the obviously heraldic images in the colour/animal combination of the White Horse, probably representing the House of Hanover, and the Red Lion, most often showing a link to Scotland. The Snowdrop shows an image of what is regarded as the first flower of spring. It may also be heraldic, although who and what it represents is unclear.

The Bent Arms was a 16th century coaching inn, the name most likely derived from a surname associated with the place. In the 1980s the Linden Tree was aptly named, the large tree towering over the front door the perfect marker. However, in 2005, following extensive refurbishment, the place was renamed the Stand Up Inn. Perhaps the owners had skimped on the budget and not included seats? No, there are indeed plenty of seats today, but not in the 1800s when it was first built. No seats gave the pub its original name of the Stand Up Inn.

Littlehampton

Recorded as simply Hantone in 1086, it is not until 1482 that we first find Lyttelhampton. From Old English *ham tun* the original name referred to 'the home farm' with the later addition of 'smaller' thought to distinguish this from Southampton in neighbouring Hampshire.

Pub names derived from its location near the sea are common enough. The Dolphin is an image featured in the coat of arms of the Fishmongers' Company and also the Company of Watermen and Lightermen. Wherever this appears it most often refers to the mammal seen as a friend and good omen by sailors. The Steam Packet was named after the type of vessel, the Marine Hotel speaks for itself, and probably the most famous English mariner gave his name to the Nelson Hotel. Not only the sea is nearby but the estuary of the River Arun. This leads to the name of the Arun View Inn, where the scene invariably includes a pair of swans, hence the name of the Cob and Pen.

Six Bells is a religious link, usually meant to show the number of bells in the nearby belfry but was often inaccurate. The Locomotive is named for its proximity to the railway station and is found on Terminus Road. The New Inn is found in just about every town in the country, although very few are still 'new' and thus 'newer' might have been a better idea when these were opened. A tongue-in-cheek welcome is offered to all by the name of the Dewdrop Inn, the same message is the basis for the name of the Globe Inn where all are welcome. While the phrase 'true blue' would suggest a Conservative supporter today, historically it applied to a Scottish Presbytarian or anyone who wished to distinguish themselves from the red associated with royalty.

The Crown is clearly showing support for the monarchy and thus the nation. Patriotic names are always plentiful. The Britannia Inn is the most obvious, a

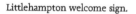

Littlehampton welcome sign.

The Steam Packet public house, Littlehampton.

female figure seen on pre-decimal coinage and on medals for many years. The image is based on Frances Stewart, mistress of Charles II who later became Duchess of Richmond. The Regent House honours the Prince Regent, George Augustus Frederick, son of George III who was incapable of ruling owing to his insanity. He later ruled in his own right as George IV, however, he was almost universally loathed as a person, as regent, and as King. Not named after the monarchs of the House of Hanover, or indeed later, the George takes the name of the patron saint of England. The Gratwicke Arms is named after a man who held the title of High Sheriff of Sussex. There were two of this name who held this position for a year: John Gratwicke in 1694 and William Gratwicke in 1772.

Lodsworth

Domesday records this name as Lodesorde in 1086. Here the Saxon personal name is followed by Old English *worth* and describes 'the enclosure of a man called Lod'.

Gallows Hill speaks for itself, where the old Liberty of Lodsworth executed its criminals. Redlands Farm comes from Middle English *ridde* referring to 'the cleared lands'.

The Halfway Bridge Inn is aptly named as near a bridge over the river and equidistant on the road between Midhurst and Petworth. The Hollist Arms remembers the family who were associated with the village from 1312 until the 20th century.

Lurgashall

A name which appears as Lutegareshale in a 12th century document. This record is little different from the Old English *lute gar halh* and thus we can be certain this is describing 'the nook of land with a trapping spear'.

Minor names begin with Barfold, from *burh falod* this is probably representing 'the pen or fold of the manor' rather than 'the fold of the fortified place'. Benefold Copse tells of 'the pen or fold of a man called Benna'. Brocklehurst Farm comes from *brock hyrst* 'the wooded hill frequented by badgers'. Chillinghurst adds *hyrst* to a Saxon personal name to recall this as 'the wooded hill of a man called Cilla'. Similarly Diddlesfold Farm describes 'the pen or fold of a man called Dyddel'.

Locals can enjoy a drink at the Noah's Ark, an image found in the coat of arms of the Shipwright's Company.

Lyminster

The earliest surviving record of this name comes from the late ninth century and as Lolinminstre in *Domesday*. Here the Saxon personal name is suffixed by Old English *ing mynster* and tells of 'the large church associated with a man called Lulla'.

Batworthpark House began life as 'the *worth* or enclosure of a man called Baeda', later the addition of 'park' tells us it was an area sectioned off with the later addition of the building of the house. Toddington is easy to see as a Saxon personal name with Old English *inga tun* and telling of 'the farmstead of the family or followers of a man called Totta'. Calcetto Priory took its name from the causeway built by the monks to provide access between the castle and its town with the high ground on the opposite side of the valley.

Madehurst

A name recorded as Medliers in 1188 and as Medhurst in 1255. There are two equally possible Old English origins for this name, either *maed hyrst* and 'the wooded hill near the meadow land' or *maethel hyrst* and 'the assembly place at or by the wooded hill'.

Marden (East, North & West)

The basic name here comes from Old English *gemaere dun* and tells of 'the boundary hill'. Listed as simply Meredone in the *Domesday* record of 1086, the additions are self-explanatory.

Locksash is a local name describing 'the wooded hill of a man called Locc'. The Victoria Inn commorates the 64 year reign of the Queen who would have been announced as: 'Her Majesty Victoria, by the Grace of God, of the United Kingdom of Great Britain and Ireland, Queen, Defender of the Faith, Empress of India'.

Medway, River

Records of this name include Fluminis Meduuuaeian in 764 (surely the only example of a place name with seven consecutive vowels!) and as Aqua de Medewey in 1279. If the first element is a Celtic *medu*, which has a common origin with Saxon *mere*, then it is highly likely the suffix is found in the name of the Wye, a river name found more than once in England and Wales and together speak of 'the river sweet with water'.

Merston

Domesday records this name as Mersitone in 1086. This is from *mersc tun*, Old English for 'the farmstead on marshy ground'.

Local names include Banwell Farm, from *bean wielle* meaning 'the stream near where beans are grown'. With the suffix *leah* Bowley Farm tells of 'the woodland clearing of a man called Bofa'. With Brinfast Farm the suffix is *faesten* and telling of 'the stronghold of a man called Bryni'.

Runcton adds *inga tun* to a Saxon personal name and means 'the farmstead of the family or followers of a man called Run'. Saltham Farm is the location of former salt workings. Vinnetrow Farm describes itself as 'the tree of the fen dwellers', a lone tree in this flat landscape would be very obvious. Camic Pond tells it was 'where cammock or restharrow grows', a member of the onion family which is traditionally used to treat bladder and kidney problems.

The Kings Head depicts an image of the king of diamonds on its sign. Here is an example of the name showing support for the monarchy in general rather than one specific individual.

Middleton on Sea

A very common place name which, as here, is normally found with a distinguishing addition. Here that addition is not seen until the 19th century, compared to others this is very late. The basic name is first seen in 1086 as

Middeltone, the *Domesday* record showing this is *middel tun* and describing 'the middle farmstead', a reference to its location between two others.

Elmer Farm comes from Old English *el mere* 'the pool frequented by eels'.

Midhurst

Found as Middeherst in 1186, this name comes from Old English *midd hyrst* and 'the middle wooded hill'. Whiphill features a personal name and Old English *hyll*, telling of 'the hill of a man called Wippa'.

Street names begin with The Mint, a reminder of the Midhurst Farthings, a local issue as low denomination currency was in short supply and doing so prevented prices being inflated. Lion Street is a reminder of the Red Lion Inn. Wool Lane and Sheep Lane are obviously places where the wool trade flourished. However, the latter, Sheep Lane, was previously known as Hog Lane, not a pig but a term describing a sheep which has yet to be shorn.

Duck Lane is a corruption of the earlier Dyke Lane, showing there was a ditch along here. Wetters Lane led to the town's water meadows. Kempes Corner remembers the name of a former tenant. Knockhundred Row has more explanations than all the rest of the streets combined, however, none are worth repeating as they are all clearly examples of creative etymology.

The Wheatsheaf has been a common pub name since the 17th century. Its origins are certainly heraldic, although whether this particular example is from the Worshipful Company of Bakers, the Brewers' Company, or one of several other bodies is uncertain. Similarly the Unicorn is an heraldic representation of Scotland. The Greyhound most likely a reminder of the dukes of Newcastle, major landholders.

The Silver Horseshoe is from an heraldic image, possibly related to the Tudor building of Cowdray Castle. The Half Moon Inn uses an easily reproduced image, albeit one which shows a crescent moon. The Swan took the image of the bird which has been a permanent sight on the River Rother for centuries. The Crown shows this establishment was run by a patriot and a royalist.

It is clear a horse has four legs and thus requires four shoes, therefore the name of the Three Horse Shoes should be seen as a question and the blacksmith alongside the inn offering a solution to the missing shoe. The Bricklayers Arms shows not only metalworkers but builders were important local trades.

Mundham

Listed as Mundhame in 692 and as Mundreham in 1086, the suffix here is difficult to define and could be Old English *ham* or *hamm* following the Saxon personal name. Thus this name is seen as describing either 'the homestead of a man called Munda' or 'the hemmed-in land of a man called Munda'.

Newtimber

Listed as Nitimbre in 950, Niuembre in 1086, and as Newetymber in 1270, there is no doubt this is from Old English *niwe timber* and that it refers to an early lumber yard.

Locally Saddlescombe literally describes 'the valley of the saddle', a reference to the topography.

North Chapel

A name which hardly seems to require an explanation, except to say it is historically north of and associated with Petworth. This is a surprisingly recent name, the first surviving record dates from 1514, much more recent than the following minor place names.

Those names include Colhook Common, describing 'the hook of land of a man called Cola', while Stilland Farm comes from Old English *stigel* which has evolved to become 'stile' but was once also used to describe the path on which it stood.

A source of fresh water may not seem the biggest attraction when advertising a pub name, for a pub sign, and thus its name, is effectively an advertisement. Yet when the Deepwell Inn was named it showed just that, a reliable source of fresh water exists here. Whilst drinkable fresh water was important, the real reference here is to the quality of the beer then brewed on site.

North Stoke

Recorded as Stoches in the *Domesday* census of 1086 and as Norstok for the first time in 1253, the addition of 'north' describes its position in relation to South Stoke. Old English *stoc* should correctly be described as 'special place' although, of course, what was special in Saxon terms may not seem quite as important today. In fact, the Saxon understanding of 'special' was not as we would understand it today, they were simply stating this was used for a specific purpose, something so mundane they never saw fit to record just what that purpose was.

Nutbourne

Listed as Nordborne in 1086, the *Domesday* record points to Old English *north burna* or 'the northern stream'. However, there are later records from the 13th century as Notburn and Neoburna, which point to *hnutu burna* or 'the stream where nuts can be gathered'. So which is correct?

Normally the earlier the record the more reliable, if for no other reason than those who recorded the name either spoke or understood the language of the Saxons, Old English, and while the phonetic spelling may be a little confusing the chances are these forms will offer the best clues. By the time of the 13th century, as in the case of these later examples, Old English was well on the way to becoming Middle English and, while the two are not overly different, a misunderstanding could easily have mistaken 'nut' for 'north' and *vice versa*.

However, here the early record is *Domesday* which, while undoubtedly an excellent source of information on late 11th century England, is a notoriously unreliable source of proper names. Be they place names or personal names the Normans had a problem with Saxon names, which comes as no surprise considering their history. Both are a part of the Indo-European group of languages which, for our purposes, split into two groups in western Europe: the Germanic, which resulted in German, Swedish, Norwegian, Danish, Dutch, and of course English, with the Latin arm giving French, Spanish, Portuguese, Italian, Latin and Romansh. If we consider the differences between the English spoken on this side of the Atlantic when compared with that on the American side of that ocean, and remember here we are speaking the same language, it is surprising the census was completed as quickly as it was.

If the two cultures, at least linguistically, had little in common, it raises the questions as to how reliable the rest of the information is and how they ever managed to produce this document? The answer is simply the Normans quickly learned the words which are repeated again and again in *Domesday*: acre, pig, eels, ploughs, virgate, honey, and the like form the basis of every entry. Indeed the only thing that really changes are the proper names, which is why we find so many discrepancies. While experts have learned, to some degree, to see how scribes have produced a Saxon name with the phonetic spelling of a French accent (very useful when *Domesday* is our only early source) it still makes the great tome a frustrating source when defining place names. Returning to our original question, the correct one must be 'the stream where nuts may be gathered'.

Pubs include the Rising Sun, the image of the dawn has been used in heraldry since at least the reign of Edward III. It is also seen in the arms of Richard III and many influential families. The Barley Corn is a reference to the plant used to produce the malt used in the brewing process.

Nuthurst

Found as Nothurst in 1228, this comes from the Old English *hnutu hyrst* 'the wooded hill where nut trees grow'.

Sedgewick Castle was built on land which was already described as 'the *wic* or specialised farm by where sedge grows'. The Black Horse has been chosen by many families as a device in their coat of arms, including the Percival family of neighbouring Hampshire.

Nyetimber

The earliest surviving record of this name dates from the 12th century as Neuetunbra. This is from Old English *niwe timbre* and describes 'the new timbered building'.

Nyton

Listed as the modern form as early as 1327, this is probably 'the new farmstead' from Old English *niwe tun*. However, there is a chance this is a shortened form of *atten ieg tun* and thus 'at the farmstead of the dry ground in a marsh'.

Offham

This name comes from Old English *woh hamm* and tells of 'the crooked hemmed-in land'. The name is recorded as Wocham at the end of the 11th century.

Oving

A name seen in 956 as Uuinges is from an Old English *inga* and a Saxon personal name and describes the '(place of) the family or followers of a man called Ufa'.

Here we find Colworth, 'the *worth* or enclosure of a man called Cola'; 'the farmstead at the portage' is from *draeg tun*, seen in the common name of Drayton; Shopwyke is from *sceap wic* 'the farm specialising in sheep'; and Woodhorn Farm stands on 'the wooded nook of land'.

The Gribble Inn is named after a fruit. This small, yellow-skinned apple was grown here, the name first noted in 1831.

P

Pagham

Listed as Pecganham in 680 and as Pageham in 1086, this name features the common combination of a Saxon personal name and Old English *ham* giving 'the homestead of a man called Paecga'.

Local names include Aldwick, referring to 'the old specialised farm', that speciality is nearly always dairy produce. Crimsham began life as 'the *ham* or homestead of a man called Crymi'. The early records of Honer show this was originally from *holh ora fleot* telling of 'the hollow bank at the tidal creek'.

Lagness points to an origin of *lang esc* 'the long stubble land'. The name of Nyetimber comes from *niwe timber* literally 'the new timber' but which should be seen as a newer woodyard. Sefter Farm is from *seohtre*, a name telling us this was alongside a 'drain, ditch'. Willowhale Farm was worked 'at the nook of land where willow grows'.

With an heraldic sign showing it is associated with the dukes of Norfolk, whose family seat is at Arundel, the White Lion remains a popular pub name. Another strong image is that of the bear and features in the arms of many leading families. However, that the Bear at Pagham does not have a colour

Pagham village sign.

The Lamb Inn, Pagham, shows an association with the church.

assigned to it points more to a reference to the barbaric 'sport' or bear-baiting, not banished in England until 1835. Another animal, or rather its image, hangs outside the Lamb. Here is yet another area, this showing a religious connection for the Lamb of God was used to refer to Jesus Christ.

Parham

A name found as Perham in a document dated 959, there is little dispute this is from Old English *pirige ham* and giving 'the homestead where pears grow'.

Locally the name of Pope's Lane remembers John Pope, here by 1628.

Patching

Derived from a Saxon personal name and Old English *inga*, this name tells of the '(place of) the family or followers of a man called Paecci'. Records of this name include Paeccingas in 960 and as Petchings in 1086.

Barnstake Copse is from Old English *bern stocc*, a very specific description of 'the place marked by stocks or tree stumps cleared by burning'. World's End is a minor name which belongs to the group known as 'remoteness' names. These are found from anywhere after the 15th century and represent the humour of the day. The land associated with a village or parish cannot be a perfect circle centred on the main part of the village, thus there is always a part which is farthest away, requiring a longer travelling time in each direction in order to work the land. These were given names which suggested they were even more distant and usually named after faraway places in the news at the time. Hence we find Botany Bays, New Zealands, Californias and here the World's End which is now only seen in the name of the pub. The Fox is a popular name most often chosen for its image as much as its reputation. Stabling and refreshment for horse and rider are advertised by the name of the Horse and Groom.

Pease Pottage

Another comparatively recent name, this is first seen in 1724 when recorded as Peaspottage Gate. This is probably a reference to 'a gap or gate on soft or muddy ground'.

Petworth

Recorded as Peteorde in 1086, the *Domesday* record adds Old English *worth* to a Saxon personal name and speaks of 'the enclosure of a man called Peota'.

Local street names begin with Bartons Lane, which has been said to be derived from the 18th-century resident John Barton. However, the name seems to be much older. It was previously known as Cragg Lane after the Cragg family who lived at Wisteria Cottage and who provided services to the locals as painters, plumbers and glaziers. It seems likely the Barton family replaced the Craggs.

Angel Street is derived from the Angel Inn. Grove Street was known as World's End until the 1860s, a common name for a far flung corner of a parish. The road name comes from its destination, itself marked as New Grove on maps until the 1860s. Hence the name describes 'the small woodland'.

Some street names are of obvious derivation. Here we find North Street, Church Street, Park Road, East Street, Middle Street, High Street, Market Square, Saddlers Row, and Station Road. Such names are found in almost every town, or at least were at some time. We also find Pound Street, a place where stray animals were impounded awaiting collection by their owner on payment of the fine. Note New Street here is only about 200 years old, making it one of the 'newest' of New Streets.

Here is Bennyfold Farm which began as 'the pen or enclosure of a man called Bynna', the same *fold* is seen in the name of 'the pen or enclosure near the beech trees'. From *pytt falod* comes Petsalls Copses, 'the pen or enclosure by a pit'.

Brinksole features the suffix *syle* referring to 'the miry or muddy place of a man called Brynca'. What began as 'the spur of land of a man called Cuthhere' is still on the map as Coultershaw Bridge. Kelsham tells of 'the homestead of a man called Cyllis', and Elkham Farm comes from 'the *ham* or homestead of a man called Ylca'. From Old English *haesel ing burna* comes Haslingbourne, the 'stream associated with where hazel trees grow'.

Hoes Farm comes from the plural of *hoh*, telling of 'the spurs of land'. Horsebear is derived from *hors baere* 'the woodland pasture where horses are grazed'. Ratford Farm was laid out alongside 'the reedy ford'. Banniards Copse, a reminder the family of Bartholomew Baynard was here in the 13th century. The name of Shimmings features a dialect word for 'a hoe', land which was regularly worked with a hoe at a time when it was not in general use.

Pub names here include the Star, a religious link which symbolises the Virgin Mary. A more obvious religious image is seen in the Angel Inn. The Lickfold Inn takes a place name coming from *hlinc fald* or 'the fold or pen for animals at the ridge of land'. The Cricketers shows this was where locals formed a team to participate in the national summer sport.

Imagery is the only reason for the name of the Half Moon Inn; instantly recognised, it also hints at the hours after dark when most are likely to visit the local. Known as the Railway until 1873, thankfully someone suggested renaming the pub on the Mitford Estate the Three Moles Inn. As can be seen from the sign the name is derived from the crest of the Mitford family which features three of these small mammals on the shield.

Another heraldic image is seen outside the Black Horse Inn. Used by many it can be found on the letterheads of a well-known bank, was the nickname of the 7th Dragoon Guards, and represented the goldsmiths of Lombard Street in London. The Stag Inn is another popular image, most often this can be traced back to the hunt. Perhaps the Stonemason's Inn is an indication this was where such a craftsman retired having made his fortune. The Welldiggers Arms is unlikely to refer to those who physically dug a well, simply a reference to a pub with a supply of fresh water.

Plaistow

Listed as La Pleyestowe in 1271, here is 'the place for play or sport' derived from Old English *pleg stow*.

Polling

Listed as Palinges in 1199, here a Saxon personal name and Old English *inga* combine to tell of the '(place of) the family or followers of a man called Puna'.

Poynings

Found in 960 as Puningas and as Poninges in 1086, here a Saxon personal name and Old English *inga* and describes the '(place of) the family or followers of a man called Puna'.

Pulborough

A name derived from the Old English *pol beorg* which refers to 'the pool by the hill or mound'. The name is recorded as Poleberge in the *Domesday* record of 1086.

Local names include Brinsbury Farm, referring to 'the *burh* or fortified place of a man called Bryni'; Codmore Farm tells of 'the *mere* or pool of a man called Codda'; Frithwoods comes from Old English *fyrhth* 'sparse woodland'; Guildenhurst Farm is from *gylden hyrst* 'the golden wooded hill', the colour describes its autumnal appearance.

Homestreet Farm puts together Middle English *holm* and Old English *strica*, literally 'the stroke of holly', where stroke refers to a strip of land. Rawstick Farm is from *ruh stocc* or 'the rough land marked by stocks or stumps'. Rowner features the same first element, here with *ora* and speaking of 'the rough bank of land'. Finally Streele Farm comes from *strael* 'the straight (way)'.

Public houses here include the Five Bells, a reference to the church and while often thought to refer to the number of bells in the belfry this is rarely the case. The Anchor is another link to the church, although the nearby sea cannot be entirely ruled out. While the Oddfellows Arms shows this was a meeting place for the Independent Order of Oddfellows, a benevolent society founded in the 19th century.

Both the patriot, in the form of the rose, and the royalist, represented by the crown, are shown in the name of the Rose and Crown. The Swan is probably another royal device, it being found in the arms of both Henry VIII and Edward III. Similarly the White Horse represents the House of Hanover, the ruling house in this country from 1714 to 1901.

Pyecombe

Found as Picumba in a late 11th-century document, this is from Old English *pie cumb* and describes 'the valley infested with gnats'.

Pangdean features the suffix *denu* and describes 'the valley of a man called Pinca'. A similar meaning, but this time the suffix is *cumb*, as seen in Varncombe Barm or 'the valley where bracken grows'.

R

Rackham

Recorded as Recham in 1166, this name comes from Old English *hreac hamm* and 'the hemmed-in land with hay ricks'.

Racton

The *Domesday* record of 1086 gives this as Rachetone, while by 1121 this had become Rakentune. This would seem to be a Saxon personal name Roca which, while unknown, would be the expected version of Old German Raco, Rakio, or Racca. Here with the addition of Old English *tun* giving 'the farmstead of a man called Roca'.

Local names include Gunter's Stone, recalling the name of Roger Gunetyr who was here by 1327. Lordington features Old English *inga tun* with an uncertain Saxon personal name giving 'the farmstead of the family or followers of a man called Leofraed, Leodheard, or Leodraed'.

Rake

The earliest surviving record dates from 1296 where it appears exactly as it does today. This is from Old English *hraca* and speaks of the '(place at) the pass'.

Roffey

A name which is derived from one of two Old English origins and recorded as La Rogheye in 1281. Either this is *rah hege* 'the enclosure for roe deer' or *ruh hege* 'the rough enclosure'.

The local pub is the Norfolk Arms. A reference to the largest local landholder, the dukes of Norfolk whose family seat is at Arundel.

Rogate

Listed as Ragata in the 12th century, this is from Old English *ra geat* and describes 'the gate or gap for roe deer'.

Locally we find Durford, from *deor ford* 'the ford used by animals'. It is easy to see this as also referring to 'deer ford', however, the Saxons used *deor* to refer to animals in general as much as deer. This is not as confusing as it seems, even today Hoover has become the generic term for all vacuum cleaners.

Fyning comes from *fin* probably describing 'the heaped hill', the apparent shape. The Rake comes from *racu* desribing 'the bed of the stream'. Wenham tells us it was 'the *ham* or homestead of a man called Wena'.

Rudgwick

Recorded as Regwic in a document from 1210, this is derived from Old English *hrycg wic* and referring to 'the specialised farm at the ridge'. Most likely the speciality would have been dairy produce.

Local names include Exfold Farm, which began as 'the fold for oxen'. Marles reminds us this is a place 'where marl was dug'. Naldrett House is from *atten alder* 'the place at the clump of alder trees'. Rowhook is from Old English *ruh hoc* meaning 'the rough hook of land'. Lastly, defining Wanford Bridge paints a virtual picture of life in earlier times, this describing 'the ford crossed by waggons'.

The Wheatsheaf is an image seen in several coats of arms, most notably the Brewers' Company and the Worshipful Company of Bakers. In a small community the landlord could often offer both bread and beer to his customers. Charles II is the image on the sign outside the Kings Head, although the name is a more general show of support for the monarchy.

Runcton

A name featuring a Saxon personal name and Old English *ing tun* and referring to 'the farmstead associated with a man called Hrica'. The name appears as Rochintone in the *Domesday* record of 1086.

The Walnut Tree was taken for a pub name as, like the vast majority of 'tree' names, it provided a large and almost permanent marker for the premises.

Rusper

Found as Rusparre in 1219, this comes from Old English *ruh spearr* and describes the '(place at) the rough spar or beam of wood'.

Early records of Faygate do not clarify whether this is *feo hege* 'the fence enclosing the area for cattle' or *rah hege* 'the deer fence'. In the second case the fence would have been a barrier to deer, there also being a word *hlip* which describes a lower fence which allowed the passage of deer but served as a barrier to livestock. Early forms of Puckscroft show this was taken from the nearby *puca dun* 'the hill of the goblin'. From Old English *stane mere ham* Stammerham Farm describes the location of 'the homestead by the stony pool'.

Two of the most popular pub names in the land are found at Rusper, the Royal Oak recalling the time in 1651 when Charles II hid in a tree, thereafter referred to as the Royal or Boscobel Oak, to escape the Parliamentarian forces in hot pursuit. The Plough has been a common name since the 16th century, a time when almost everyone earned a living from the land. Here the message is clear, this establishment is open to all. Some pubs still hang a replica in place of a painted sign, much as the early pubs would have.

Two other pubs share a theme, although the Star Inn and the Lamb may seem quite unrelated. It is easier to see the star as associated with religion, the most obvious image that of the Star of Bethlehem and it is this event which did lead to the star being the heraldic representation of the Virgin Mary. It is through this heraldic image the pub is most often named. Similarly the Lamb is religious and representative of the Son of God. This link between the church and the demon drink may seem odd today, however, once these were the only two places where a community would gather in any numbers and the pub may well be on church land.

Rustington

Seen as Rustinton in 1180, this tells of 'the farmstead associated with a man called Rusta' where the Saxon personal name and Old English *ing tun*.

Locals can enjoy a drink at the Windmill Inn, both it and Mill Lane where it is located are named after a former mill. The Lamb Inn, as seen under the entry for Rusper, is a religious name and representative of the Son of God.

S

Salvington

Found in a document from 1249 as Saluinton, this features a Saxon personal name and Old English *ing tun* and speaks of 'the farmstead associated with a man called Saelaf or Saewulf'.

Selham

This comes from Old English *sele ham* and refers to 'the farmstead by a copse of sallow trees' and is recorded in the *Domesday* survey of 1086 as Seleham.

Snapelands Copse comes from *snaep* 'boggy land' and *land* 'cultivated land', together this is understood as showing how the former boggy land was drained.

Selsey

Listed as Seolesiae at the beginning of the eighth century and as Selesie in *Domesday*, this name comes from old English *seolh eg* and refers to 'the island of the seal'. Locally we find the name of Selsey Bill, itself not seen before the 18th century and with the addition representing Old English *bile* 'a beak or bill' a reference to this promontory.

Selsey's coastline.

We should expect to find Selsey Bill to be a bill or beak-shaped prominence as is the case with other coastal places of this name. It seems this can only have been named to mirror such places, such as Portland Bill, for there is no suggestion of any such shape for the point of land here.

Selsey welcomes us with a wave.

Medmerry Farm has two elements, *medeme* 'of moderate size, medium' and *ig* 'dry land in marsh, island'. Norton is easily seen as 'the northern *tun* or farmstead', we also know what it was north of, for there was once a Sutton. The Dobbin features a dialect word for sea gravel mixed with sand.

Selsey's name tells us it is virtually surrounded by water, so no surprise to find pubs referring to such in the Lifeboat and the Fisherman's Joy. Clearly a royalist and a patriot suggested the name of the Crown Inn.

However, the author's favourite pub name here is the Stargazer. During the 18th century a stargazer was a slang term for a woman of ill-repute, otherwise known as a hedge whore. Both terms referred to how she shunned brothels (and thus the cut from her earnings) in favour of a road-side location and describes her view while at work. The term was also used as recently as the 20th century to describe a certain part of the male anatomy which could, at certain times, be seen to extend much as a telescope extends to increase the focal length. However, the real reference, and why it is one of the author's favourites, is to honour Selsey's most famous resident, one of the great characters of the modern era and the man who introduced us to the wonders of the universe, Sir Patrick Moore.

Shermanbury

A name recorded as Syremanebir in 1235 and as Schirmanebury in 1271, this is a place name describing 'the stronghold of the shireman'. Here is Old English *burh scireman*, with this a local official or steward.

We should point out there is an earlier form of the name, *Domesday* records this as Salmonesberie in 1086. However, the idea of this being 'the stronghold of the salmon', even if this is being used as a personal name, can be discounted for the reasons explained in detail under the entry for Nutbourne.

Local names include Sakeham Farm, in Saxon times it was known as 'the *ham* or homestead of a man called Sacca'.

Shipley

Records of this name include Scapeleia in 1073 and as Sepelei in 1086. A name found in several places in England and always from Old English *sceap leah* and telling of 'the woodland clearing where sheep are kept'.

Minor names of the area include Knepp Castle, from *cnaep* meaning 'hillock', an obvious place for a fortification. Pondtail Farm is easy to see when defined as 'the lower end of the pool or stream'. Smithers hill comes from *smethe worth* or 'the enclosure on the level or smooth place'. St Joan's Farm was associated with the Prior of the Hospital of St John of Jerusalem.

The oddly named Dragons would be difficult to define were it not for a legend passed down through the ages. A dragon was held to be abroad in the forest, everyone was afraid until St Leonard arrived and slew the beast, the wood thereafter known as St Leonard's Forest. It is said that wherever the blood of the dragon fell lilies would blossom.

This mythical beast returns in the name of the pub the George and Dragon. Here we find the patron saint of England and his most famous deed. The Countryman offers a welcome to everyone.

Shoreham by Sea

Found as Sorham in 1073 and as Soreham in 1086, this name comes from Old English *scora ham* and describes 'the homestead by a steep slope'. The addition of 'by Sea' was not seen until the Victorians made seaside holidays popular. Old Shoreham refers to that part of the town built before the arrival of the Normans.

Street names of Shoreham include those named after local figures. Colonel Colvill Bridger JP lived at Buckingham House, a 19th-century landowner remembered by Colvill Avenue. Wiston House in Steyning was home to the three brothers of the Shirley family, when they were not away on their travels. Shirley Close marks their departure point of Shoreham during the 17th century.

Cecil Pashley Way forms the perimeter road of Shoreham Airport, hence it is no surprise to find the man was associated with flying. Indeed both he and his brother Eric served in the Royal Flying Corps during World War One. Sadly Eric was killed when his aircraft crashed but Cecil went on to organise flying displays, founded the local flying school, taught South African pilots during World War Two when serving at an RAF base in Rhodesia, and continued to pass on his knowledge and skills in peace time.

Mansell Road recalls merchant Francis Mansell, a name also honoured by the Sussex Yacht Club in an annual event. Both Mansell's vessel and the yachting event known as the Royal Escape mark the man's role in getting the future Charles II out of the country. Woodards View recalls Nathaniel Woodard, vicar of St Mary's in the 19th century. He played a major role in the development of local education and was instrumental in the building of Lancing College, one of 35 schools in the country funded from the Woodard Foundation.

During the Battle of Britain just one aircrew member was awarded the Victoria Cross. He was flying a Hurricane over Southampton Water when spotting several enemy planes, he engaged the Luftwaffe and let loose with many rounds of fire. His plane was also hit and yet, despite being on fire, continued to attack and brought down his target. It was only then he abandoned his aircraft and parachuted back to land on home soil. Yet Flight Lieutenant James Brindley Nicolson was met by a local Defence Volunteer (later known as the Home Guard) who shot him in the backside with his 303 Lee Enfield rifle. For both reasons Nicolson Drive is well deserved.

Gorringe Close is a fitting memorial to Lieutenant General Sir George Frederick Gorringe, commander of the 47th Division of the British Army. He saw action in Mesopotamia, the Boer Wars, and World War One. Following his retirement from the army in 1918 he settled to the life of a farmer at Shoreham and is buried at St Julian's churchyard. Local historian and founder of the Marlipins Museum, Henry Cheal, merits the naming of Cheal Close.

Gordon Road remembers General Charles George Gordon CB, who commanded the British troops in the Boxer Rebellion and was killed at the siege of Khartoum. The Burrells and also The Burrell Arms recall Charles Merrick Burrells, who was the member of parliament for Shoreham for a highly impressive 56 years. A reminder of the coaching era is seen in the name of the Royal Coach. The Green Jacket is taken from the nickname for the King's Royal Rifle Corps, which began as the cricket club formed by the 60th Foot and the Rifle Brigade.

In the churchyard of St Botolphs is the grave of one Captain Scras. He was captain of the *Dolphin*, a vessel given the royal seal to sack and loot any vessel out of a European port in order to swell the King's coffers – which not only sounds like piracy, it is piracy. The hull of the *Dolphin* was hauled ashore at the end of its sea-going days, common practice at the time, where the upturned hull made an excellent shed with copious storage space. It seems this came to rest at what is now known as Dolphin Road.

Falcon Road is named after another vessel, the *Falcon*, a 24-gun warship built at the local shipyard with a gross weight of 240 tons. The vessel was captured by the French soon after its launch and its commander, one Henry Middleton, was deemed to be wholly responsible. Brought before a court martial he was found guilty and fined three months' pay. Another vessel gave its name to Feversham Close. It was lost during the North American campaign, a victim of a huge storm with the loss of all hands. Divers have recently found the wreck on the sea bed and recovered several items.

Fowey Close recalls the 377 ton 32-gun *Fowey*, built at Shoreham. The vessel was under the command of Captain Charles Ratcliffe when taken by the French off the Scillies in 1704. The Battle of Beachy Head connects John Bembow with Sussex. Born in Shropshire, Admiral Benbow is better remembered as the subject of a sea shanty and for the name of the inn in Robert Louis Stevenson's *Treasure Island*.

View from Norfolk Bridge,
Shoreham by Sea.

Admiral Lord Nelson's misquoted dying words of 'Kiss me Hardy' were addressed to the man who gave his name to Hardy Close. Vice Admiral Thomas Masterson Hardy was the actual commander of HMS *Victory* when Nelson was mortally wounded by sniper's bullet. The commander of the *Royal Sovereign* at the Battle of Trafalgar was Vice Admiral Cuthbert Collingwood, hence the name of Collingwood Court.

Other ocean-related names include The Marlinspike, a tool used on board ship, traditionally for splicing ropes but which could be put to other uses. Mariners prided themselves on their skill with the Marlinspike. Flag Square is a reminder of how messages could be communicated via systems such as semaphore between vessels and/or the shore.

The nobility are always a popular choice for a street name. Connaught Avenue refers to Prince Arthur, Duke of Connaught and Earl of Sussex, the seventh of Queen Victoria's children. Clarendon Road remembers Edward Hyde, 1st Earl of Clarendon who supported Charles I in the English Civil War, accompanied the future Charles II during his Paris exile, and aided the King at the Restoration of the Monarchy. Another who aided the then Prince Charles while in Paris was James Butler, Marquis of Ormonde, hence the name of Ormonde Way.

Brunswick Road remembers the wife of George IV, previously known as Caroline of Brunswick. Victoria Road needs no explanation for hardly a town or city in the land does not have a road named after the monarch who reigned from 1837 to 1901. Another consort gave her name to Adelaide Square, Queen Adelaide of Saxe Meiningen, wife of William IV is the same person who gave her name to the Australian city. Winterton Way remembers former member of parliament Edward Turnour, 6th Earl of Winterton, who officially opened the footbridge in 1921. Williams Road recalls Sir William Peare Williams, member of parliament for Shoreham in 1760 who fought to have a permanent exit to the sea from the Adur.

The Bridge Inn, Shoreham by Sea.

Hebe Road was named after the public house, itself taking the name of a 32-gun warship built locally. Ropewalk is found in many towns, it marks a long straight street where the rope could be plaited and wound from scratch. Erringham Farm comes from Old English *inga ham* with a Saxon personal name referring to this as 'the homestead of the family or followers of a man called Erra'.

Pubs include the Buckingham Arms, showing the extent of this landowning family since the title was first created in the middle of the 15th century. A century earlier a board game was played known as merels, an Old French word referring to the 'counters' each of the two players played with. While correctly called merels the name has become corrupted over and over again, known as Nine Men's Morris and, as seen in the local pub name, as Marlipins in Shoreham.

The Crown and Anchor is an apt name for a place near the coast, this being the badge seen on the sleeve of the petty officers of the Royal Navy, and symbolising the Lord High Admiral of the fleet. The Bridge Inn tells of its position before the crossing point and takes the road heading west. Similarly the name of the Ferry Inn shows another way to cross the estuary. Other names reflecting their coastal position here are the Waterside and also the Crabtree Inn.

The present building known as the Swiss Cottage refers to what was here before the development. The Swiss Gardens Primary School and Swiss Gardens road are further reminders of the Swiss Gardens. However, the present building known as the Amsterdam is very reminiscent of a Dutch property.

A symbol referring to Scotland is seen in the most common pub name in the country, the Red Lion Inn. The Royal George is a reminder of the four kings of that name whose consecutive reigns saw the House of Hanover reign from 1714 to 1830. The Royal Sovereign is a name used several times for important Royal Navy vessels. The Surrey Arms refers to the dukes of Norfolk, the family with their family seat at Arundel who also hold the title, earls of Surrey.

Sidlesham

The earliest record of this name dates from 683 as Sidelesham. Here is a Saxon personal name and Old English *ham* and refers to 'the homestead of a man called Sidel'.

Almodington puts *inga tun* with a Saxon personal name to speak of 'the farmstead of the family or followers of a man called Ealhmod or Aethelmod'. From *cealf ora* comes Chalder Farm, 'the bank of land where calves are reared'; Highleigh is *heah leah* 'the high woodland clearing'; and Keynor Farm from *cyna ora* 'the bank of land where cows are grazed'. Lastly Greatham Farm and Littleham Farm share the element *hamm*, best described as 'hemmed-in land', that is with a natural barrier on three of four sides, while the first elements are self-explanatory.

As a pub name in this coastal location the Anchor most likely refers to a landlord whose previous career was related to the sea.

Singleton

Listed as Silletone in 1086 and as Sengelton in 1185, this is from Old English *sengel tun* and describes 'the farmstead by a burnt clearing'.

Collick's Copse recalls 1705 when Dorothy Collick was residing here. While the name of Yorkhurst hill features 'the wooded hill associated with cuckoos', the very short time these birds spend in the country must cast some doubt on this explanation, hence perhaps the first element should be seen as a personal name.

The Partridge Inn is a 16th-century pub undoubtedly named for the availability of such a game bird on the menu. Perhaps this was supplied by the local poacher, or maybe that poacher (or gamekeeper) later became the landlord. However, the sign depicts the image in a different way, here the dog is accompanied by a figure in the long coat and bag associated with a poacher but that figure is not a man but a partridge. Is the bird seeking revenge?

Slaugham

A name first seen as Slacham at the end of the 11th century, this is derived from Old English *slah hamm* and describes 'the hemmed-in land where sloe or blackthorn grows'.

Dencombe tells us this was once 'the *cumb* or valley of a man called Deneca'. Warninglid is 'the leaping place of the family or followers of a man called

Waerdel', the Saxon personal name followed by Old English *inga hliep*. A leaping place can be anything which can be jumped: a bank of earth, a small stream, a marshy area, and so on. Pease Pottage tells us it was a halting place for prisoners travelling to Horsham Gaol.

The Half Moon public house actually features a sign showing a crescent moon. This is very common and while modern signs are merely the painter's personal interpretations of the name they may also be copied from earlier images, which could well be closer to the original reason for naming the establishment. Most often the half moon simply represents the night, a time when most people frequent the pub. However, it is also a common device in heraldry, although how it is represented is very important. If shown lying on its back similar to a horseshoe it represents the Turks, a likely indication the family had ancestors who went on a Crusade to the Holy Land. In English families the most common is a crescent moon with the horns dexter (pointing to the right) which indicates the second son of a family.

Slindon

Seen as Eslindone in 1086, the *Domesday* record points to an Old English origin of *slinu dun* and speaks of 'the sloping hill'.

Gumber Farm has changed somewhat since it began as 'the *worth* or enclosure of a man called Guma'.

Slinfold

Listed as Stindefald in 1165 and as Sclinfald in 1271, here we are likely looking at a union of Old Swedish *slind* and Old English *fald* giving 'the fold for animals on the slope'.

Locally we find Clemsfold, the name describing 'the fold or pen of a man called Climpe'. Dedisham also features a personal name, this being 'the homestead of a man called Daeddi'. Hurlands comes from *hyrne* or 'disused land in a river bend'. Old English *hlid wic* is seen today as Lydwicke, the 'specialised or dairy farm on a slope'. The name of Pinkhurst describes 'the *hyrst* or wooded hill of a man called Pinca'.

The most common pub name in the country is the Red Lion, no surprise when most indicate such premises had a link to Scotland. However, here we find one of just two examples of this name being found as Red Lyon. The Spur takes a local place name, it referring to a spur of land. The Newburgh Arms remembers former landowner the Earl of Newburgh.

Sompting

Found as Suntinga in 956 and as Saltinges in 1086, this name comes from Old English *sumpt inga* and describes the '(place of) the dwellers of the marshland'.

The local name of Cokeham was once a separate settlement known as 'the *ham* or homestead of a man called Cocca'.

At Sompting locals enjoy a pint, or drink of choice, in the Marquis of Granby, a surprisingly common and very widespread name which suggests it has nothing to do with Granby, some seven miles east of Nottingham. The man in question is John Manners (1721–70), Colonel of the Royal Regiment of Horse Guards by 1758, Commander-in-Chief of the British Army from 1786, and a man history records as among the most popular ever soldier to wear the British Army uniform. His courage made him immensely popular. He most oft-repeated the act of riding at the head of his men as they charged the French at the Battle of Warburg. He urged his horse on at such a speed that not only his hat but his wig were blown from his head. His name appeared outside every pub set up by him to provide a comfortable retirement from the army for very many of his men, hence its popularity.

The Gardeners Arms is heraldic, probably showing a link to an earlier career as a former landlord. The Ball Tree Inn, sadly now demolished following a

Marquis of Granby, Sompting.

disastrous fire in early 2011, probably got its name as the site of a tree where local farmers would gather for an outdoor ball.

South Stoke

A name found in the *Domesday* pages of 1086 as Stoches, with Sudstoc in 1242 the next significant form. Here is Old English *stoc* which is 'special place' but, as discussed under North Stoke, is simply a site put to a specific purpose. North Stoke is also relevant as both places were named for their relevant directions in respect to one another.

The Black Rabbit is an unusual, possibly unique, pub name. Rabbits are not indigenous to this country, being brought here for their meat and fur by the Normans during the 12th or 13th centuries. It has been suggested the colour is the result of the vast tonnage of coal brought alongside the pub by barges on the Wey & Arun Canal but this seems unlikely. While the image on the sign rarely offers much of a clue as to origins, heraldic imagery being the exception, it should be noted the black rabbit depicted does look much more like a hare.

Southwick

A simple name to define and derived from Old English *suth wic* this is 'the southern specialised farm'. Here that speciality would almost certainly have been dairy produce. The name is found as Sudewic in 1073.

Stane Street

A name easily seen as meaning 'the stony street', a street clearly surfaced as a Roman road.

Stedham

Listed as Steddanham in 960 and as Stedeham in 1086, there are two possible Old English origins for each of the elements found in this place name. As usual with such a suffix it is difficult to tell if this is *ham* or *hamm*, however, the former does lend itself better to a personal name and the latter fits better with the animal. Hence this is most likely either 'the homestead of a man called Stedda' or 'the hemmed-in land of the stallions'.

Inholms Copse literally means 'intake holly copse'. A name which should be seen as a former copse where holly grew in abundance alongside an area taken to add to existing agricultural land. Minsted comes from *minte stede* or 'the place where mint grows'. From *sliete hyrst* comes Slathurst, describing 'the muddy place at the wooded hill'.

The Hamilton Arms is a pub which remembers the family who had estates both here and at Iping.

Steyning

Found in the late ninth century as Staeningum and as Staninges in *Domesday*, again there is more than one possible Old English origin for this name. If this represents a Saxon personal name and *inga* then this would give the '(place of) the family or followers of a man called Stan'. Alternatively this could be *stan ingas* and tell of 'the dwellers at the stony place' or even from *staening* a plural term simply describing 'the stony places'.

Gatewick House was built at what used to be 'the farm where goats are reared'. Huddlestone Farm was already known as 'the farmstead of a man called Hudel' before the modern addition of 'farm'. Wappingthorn Farm describes the '(place of) the people of the thorn tree associated with a man called Waeppa'. Heathens Burial Corner, not surprisingly, refers to an ancient burial place but also tells us it was named by a Christian community for only they would refer to non-Christians as heathens.

Only one pub name in England, the Grapes, is known to be older than that of the Chequer Inn. Brought to Britain by the Romans, a sign of this name was found by archaeologists excavating the city of Pompeii, it originated from times when a real chequerboard was hung outside. The inn-keeper's message was clear, a game similar to draughts could be enjoyed within as you enjoyed a cup. When inn-keepers later became the moneyer on the street the image of the chequerboard also became associated with money. That link has been passed down through the centuries and today the main resident at number 11 Downing Street, whose job it is to ensure the prosperity of the nation, has the title of Chancellor of the Exchequer.

The Fountain is most often a reference to a local spring, although it is also an heraldic image. No surprise to find this is a link to the Plumbers' Company, less obvious is the Master Mariners. The Star Inn, a pub which can trace its history back to the 16th century, is one of the many names showing a link to religion. While the reference to the star of Bethlehem is obvious, it more often symbolises the Virgin Mary. With their seat at nearby Arundel, the Howard family, dukes of Norfolk, have their coat of arms hanging outside the Norfolk Arms. The White Horse is most likely heraldic, an image representing the House of Hanover.

Stopham

Domesday records this name as Stopeham in 1086, here is 'the homestead of a man called Stoppa' where the Saxon personal name is followed by Old English *ham*.

Store, River

A name which came from the place name of Storrington, an example of back-formation.

Storrington

Records of this name begin with the *Domesday* listing as Storgetune in 1086. Probably derived from Old English *storc tun* this would be 'the farmstead frequented by storks'.

Minor place names here include Cootham, 'the homestead of a man called Cuda'. Fryern reminds us this was 'the agricultural land of a man called Fier'. Lastly Freeland, while it speaks for itself, has no record as to why it was free.

What is today known as the Moon was formerly known as the New Moon, the change in name is appropriate for the sign which actually depicts the full moon. The previous addition of 'new' was probably meant to indicate a rebuild of the premises, it is unfortunate the obvious misunderstanding was not seen. The Eleven Cricketers is obviously evidence the pub had its own cricket team from a very early time, while the Crown Inn shows the premises was owned and/or run by a royalist.

Stoughton

Listings of this name include Estone in 1086 and Stoctona in 1121. Here the later record shows this to be from Old English and either *stocc tun* speaking of 'the farmstead by the tree stumps' or *stoc tun* 'the farmstead at the secondary place'. The *Domesday* record suggests this was previously referred to as 'the eastern farmstead' and, if this is indeed correct, would be indicating 'an easterly secondary place'.

Stansted is a place name referring to 'the stony place' from *stan stede*. What is now known as Walderton began as 'the *tun* or farmstead of a man called Wealdhere'.

Strettington

Seen as Stratone in *Domesday* and as Estrenemetone in the 12th century, this features three Old English elements. Here *straet haeme tun* speaks of 'the farmstead of those dwelling on or by the Roman road'.

Sullington

Two possible Old English origins for this name. Either this is *sieling tun* and 'the farmstead by a copse of willow trees' or *sielling tun* 'the farmstead given as a gift'. This name is recorded as Sillinctune in 959 and as Sillintone in 1086.

Cobden Farm features Old English *denu* with a Saxon personal name and tells of 'the valley of a man called Coppa'.

Sussex

The county name is first found in a late ninth century document as Suth Seaxe, while *Domesday* refers to it as Sudsexe. Both of these early forms clearly represent Old English *suth Seaxe* and tell us of the '(territory) of the southern Saxons', relative to that of the west Saxons in what was Wessex, the east Saxons of Essex, and middle Saxons of Middlesex.

Sutton

A very common place name and hence a very simple one indeed. Here Old English *suth tun* refers to 'the southern farmstead', the name recorded as Suthtun in the earliest known record from 880. The most surprising thing here is the lack of a second distinguishing element, seemingly inevitable almost everywhere else in the country.

Local names show influence from Old English such as Collumn Hill: 'the *ham* or homestead of a man called Cola', similarly Shopham Bridge is 'the *ham* of a man called Sceobba'. However, two other names show Old Scandinavian influence, possibly showing those of Scandinavian descent recorded the name, not that they named the places. Beckhall Farm describes 'the *hagi* or hedged enclosure of a man called Becca'. While Glatting comes from *glott* meaning 'sneer', a derogatory name commenting on the abilities of the farmer or of the land he worked.

T

Tangmere

Listed as Tangemere in 1086 the modern form is found as early as 680. Indeed this still represents the original Old English perfectly, *tang mere* referring to 'the pool shaped like a pair of tongs'.

The Bader Arms public house honors the name of Group Captain Sir Douglas Robert Steuart Bader CBE, DSO & Bar, DFC & Bar, FRAeS, DL (1910-82). A member of the Royal Air Force from 1928, he crashed in December 1931 while attempting aerobatic manoeuvres. He lost both legs in the crash and came very close to losing his life. He recovered and applied to continue his career but was retired on medical grounds. However, when war broke out in 1939 his application was accepted and, despite his disability, enjoyed great success over the skies of France and in the Battle of Britain. He was forced to bail out over France in 1941 and taken prisoner, yet even with his false legs he managed several escape attempts and ended up spending the remainder of the war in the infamous Colditz Castle Prisoner of War Camp. After the war he campaigned for the disabled, this work resulted in him receiving his knighthood. His life story became a book which, when made into a film, was portrayed by Kenneth More in the film *Reach For the Sky*.

Tarring, West

This name describes the '(place of) the family or followers of a man called Teorra' where the Saxon personal name is followed by Old English *inga*. Here the addition distinguishes it from the previous entry showing this example is to the west. Note there is no alternative offered for this name, unlike its namesake above. Here the early records of Teorringas in 946 and as Terringes in 1086 show the alternative is not possible. That both have an identical basic name is through the influence of one upon the other.

The George and Dragon reunites the beast slain by England's patron saint. While the Vine is the oldest known pub name in England, used by the Romans to indicate wine was available, and later used by the Worshipful Company of Distillers in their coat of arms.

Terwick

Early forms of this place name include Tortewyk in 1271, Tertewick in 1279, Turdewyk in 1291, Tordewyke in 1296, and as Turwiche in 1615. Aside from the final example there is very little time between the other four forms, 25 years may be a generation on a human timescale but for place names this is the blink of an eye. Normally we find an evolution of a name over a number of years which enables us to see how the name has developed and it can be defined. However, here we have a collection of contemporary listings which does little to help us define this difficult name.

The most plausible origin is Old English *tord wic*, the latter is defined as 'specialised farmstead' and most often a dairy farm. Yet if the first element is *tord*, or possibly Middle English *tort* which has the same meaning, this would mean the first element refers to 'dung'. While the literal meaning of 'dung farm' is, on the face of it, perfectly sensible, it simply makes no sense. Fertiliser may be sold today, organic or chemical, but in Saxon times the dung was a by-product, albeit an important one for it was not only used to improve soil but mixed with mud to produce the daub which turned a lattice of sticks and poles from something letting in all weathers to a solid wall. It would be highly unlikely that any 'dung farm' could produce enough to make it a viable commodity for a sufficient period of time to produce a place name.

Locally we find Wakeham, a name describing 'the *ham* or homestead of a man called Waca'.

Thakeham

Listed as Taceham in 1086, the *Domesday* record points to this being 'the homestead with a thatched roof' and derived from Old English *thaca ham*.

Abingworth is a hamlet and once a distinct settlement telling of 'the *worth* or enclosure of the family or followers of a man called Abba'. Apsley Farm stands on the site of what the Saxons knew as 'the woodland clearing by the aspen trees'. Slightly different is the *leah* or woodland clearing of the Ganinges tribe'. Finally Laybrook Farm began as Laybrook, itself speaking of 'the unploughed land by a brook'.

Pubs named the White Lion began as heraldic images representing Edward IV, the earls of March and, the most likely origin here, the dukes of Norfolk.

Thorney, West

With an addition to distinguish this from a similarly named minor place name, this is from Old English *thorn eg* or 'the thorn tree island' and is recorded as Thorneg in the 11th century and as Tornei in *Domesday*.

Marker Farm is derived from *mearc ora* understood as 'the boundary shore'.

Three Bridges

A comparatively modern name and one which still means exactly what it says the '(place with) three bridges'. The earliest record of this name dates from 1613 as Le three bridges.

Tillington

Here a Saxon personal name and Old English *ing tun* tell of 'the farmstead associated with a man called Tulla'. The name is recorded as Tullington in a document from 960.

Locally we find Grittenham Farm, from *gryten ham* 'the homestead on the gravelly land'. Rotherbridge Farm is 'the bridge used by cattle' from *hryther brycg*, the river Rother is named from the bridge. Salmons Bridge has acquired the final 's' in the mistaken belief this was a personal name, the true origin refers to the pinkish colour of the bricks used in its construction. Sokenholes Farm is from *sucan* meaning 'to suck', describing hollows which collected water. Lastly we find River which, unlike the previous names, has no connection with water in any way. This name is derived from Old English *aet yfre* meaning 'at the slope'.

The Horse Guards Inn could refer to either the Life Guards or the Royal Horse Guards, known collectively as the Household Cavalry, best known for the Trooping the Colour ceremony.

Tortington

Listed as Tortinton in 1086, the *Domesday* record points to an origin of 'the farmstead associated with a man called Torhta'. Here the Saxon personal name is followed by Old English *ing tun*.

Treyford

Found as Treverde in 1086, here is 'the ford marked by a tree or with a bridge from a tree trunk' from Old English *treow ford*.

Buriton comes from Old English *bere tun*, 'the farmstead where barley is grown'.

Trotton

This name either describes 'the farmstead associated with a man called Traett' or 'the farmstead of the stepping stones'. From a Saxon personal name and Old English *ing tun* or alternatively *traeding tun*, this name appears as Traitone in *Domesday* and as Tratinton in the 12th century.

Dumpford is an odd name which seems to be speaking of 'the dammed ford'. Ripsley House comes from *risp leah* 'the woodland clearing littered with twigs and branches'.

Twineham

Recorded as Tuineam in the late 11th century, here is 'the place between the streams' from Old English *betweonan ea*.

Hickstead comes from *hiehst stede* speaking of 'the highest place'. Slipe Farm tells us it was found on 'a strip of land'.

Upwaltham

Records of this name include Waltham in 1086 and as Up Waltham in 1371. The basic name is derived from Old English *weald ham* 'the homestead in the forest', the addition of *upp* simply shows it was 'higher' than another similarly named.

No Man's Land Gate is a region where a number of trackways meet, while the tracks cross claimed land, their meeting place is not under the control of any one parish. Ide's Common takes the name of Sarah Ide, recorded here in 1666.

Walberton

Given as Walburgetone in 1086, this tells us it was 'the farmstead or village of a woman called Wealdburgh or Waldburg'. Here a Saxon or Old German personal name is suffixed by Old English *tun*.

Aviston is either 'the ford of Afa or Eafa', while Choller Farm has a corrupted second element for it began as 'Celoa's *worth* or enclosure'.

The Hollytree takes its name, as with the vast majority of pubs named after trees, from the tree outside the premises which served as a large and long-lived marker.

Walderton

The earliest record of this name dates from 1168 where it appears exactly as the modern form. Here a Saxon personal name and Old English *tun* combine to tell of 'the farmstead of a man called Wealdhere'.

Warminghurst

A name found as Werningcherch in 1188, Wormighurst in 1252, and as Weremynghirst in 1279. This is from Old English *ing hyrst* following a Saxon personal name and speaking of 'the wooded hill associated with a man called Wyrma'.

Warnham

Recorded as Werneham in 1166, there are two possible origins for this place name. Either a Saxon personal name and Old English *ham* combine to give 'the homestead of a man called Waerna' or Old English *waerna hamm* refers to 'the hemmed-in land where stallions are kept'.

Hewells Farm comes from *heah wielle* 'the high spring or stream', here 'high' refers to importance. Shiremark Farm accurately describes itself as on the boundary with neighbouring Surrey. Tickfold Farm comes from *ticcen falod* 'the fold for raising kids (young goats)'.

Pub names here include the Sussex Oak, which does indeed have a large oak tree outside as we would expect but this does not explain the addition of the county. Fewer than five miles north of here, across the border in Surrey, we find the Surrey Oak at Newdigate. Hence, each is named to distinguish from the other. The Greets Inn sign shows two individuals in a mutual greeting, however, the real origin is in a place name describing 'a gravelly place'.

Warningcamp

Listed as Warnecham in 1086, as Warnekomp in 1242, Warnecampe in 1263, and as Wernecamp in 1296, here is a name featuring a Saxon personal name and Old English *camp*. Here 'the *camp* of a man called Waerna' features a Saxon term meaning 'an enclosed piece of land', although originally it had been borrowed from the Romano-British era when it described almost the opposite, an 'open and uncultivated piece of land on the edge of the settlement'.

The corruption of the personal name to 'warning' led to this name being said to have come from its location to the east of the river, thus a look-out point where an alert or warning of the enemy's advance was sent up.

Washington

A name first seen in the middle of the 10th century as Wessingatun with the later *Domesday* record of Wasingetune. Here the Saxon personal name and Old English *inga tun* describes 'the farmstead of the family or followers of a man called Wassa'.

Minor names here include Biggen Holt, derived from a personal name but corrupted from the original 'Bida's wood'. Similiarly what began as 'the wood of a man called Trigal' has become Trickles Wood. Rowdell is derived from Old English *ruh dell* 'the rough wooded valley'. The same language gave us Rock, however, there is no stone here for this is a misunderstanding of *atter ac* which means 'at the oak' but has been pronounced as 'at the rock' leading to the modern name.

The Frankland Arms remembers Sir Thomas Edward Frankland, who served as a member of parliament in the late 18th century and as High Sheriff of Sussex in 1782. He made his fortune as a merchant, both in India and in Sussex.

Weald, The

A region documented numerous times in historical documents. Records include Andred in 755 and Andredsweald in 1018, these records showing it was originally known as 'the *weald* of a man called Andred'. The personal name is also seen in Andredesceaster, a Romano-British stronghold recorded when destroyed in 491 by Aella and Cissa. Old English *weald* refers to 'high forested land now cleared'.

Westbourne

Listed as simply Burne in *Domesday*, later we find Westbourne in 1305. Here Old English *burna* or the '(place at) the stream'. The addition was to distinguish this from Eastbourne.

Adsdean House started out as 'the *denu* or valley of a man called Aeddi'; Aldsworth also features a Saxon personal name, this being 'the *worth* or enclosure of a man called Eald'. Nutbourne is easy to see as 'the stream by the nut trees'; and Gingerbread Farm was bought in the 19th century on the proceeds earned by making gingerbread.

West Dean

From Old English *west denu* here is 'the western valley', This name is recorded as simply Dene in 1086 and as Westdene in 1291.

Chilgrove is a local name where the first element is *ceole* literally 'throat' but here, with the suffix *graf*, seen as 'the grove of trees with a gulley'. Hylters comes from Old English *heolstor* describing 'the hiding place', probably meaning it was sheltered rather than some secret sanctuary. Stapleash Farm is from *stapol ersc* or 'the wooded hill marked out by posts'. Charlston is a common English place name and thus we can be certain it has a very simple meaning, even before finding the early records showing this to be *ceorl tun* or 'the farmstead of the peasants'.

Westergate

Telling of 'the most westerly gate or gap' and derived from Old English *westerra geat*, this place is recorded as Westgate in 1230 and is named to distinguish this from Eastergate.

Westhampnett

Listed as Hentone in 1086 and as Westhamptonette in 1279, here the original name is derived from Old English *heah tun* and 'the high farmstead'. Later we see the addition of 'west', which needs no explanation, and Old French *ette* meaning 'little'.

Maudlin is the site of an old leper hospital recorded as Hospitale Sancte Marie Magdalene de Loddesdoune juxta Halnaked. Molecomb has two possible meanings, either this is 'the valley of a man called Moll' or 'the valley overrun by moles'. Valdoe is a corruption of Old English *weald geheag* 'the enclosure by the cleared forest'; Westerton speaks of 'the most westerly *tun* or farmstead'; Woodcote is from *wudu cot* 'the cottage near the wood'.

West Lavington

A name which is derived, along with Woolavington, as 'the farmstead of the family or followers of a man called Wulflaf'. As discussed under the entry for Woolavington, the present name of Lavington is a corruption, the name effectively given as 'Laf'. This is neither a pet form nor a shortened version of Wulflaf and can only be down to mispronunciation or a misunderstanding of the actual name.

That Woolavington was earlier recorded as East Lavington (see Woolavington entry for a full discussion) can only be because both that and this settlement's names had become similarly corrupted, for whatever reason. Hence the necessary addition of East and West respectively. It seems likely both places were known as 'Wulflaf's *inga tun*' and by the alternative 'Lavington' version. In this case the corruption survived, while Woolavington retained its original name.

The Royal Oak is among the most common of English pub names, this commemorating the time when Charles II and his aide Colonel Carless hid in an oak tree to escape the Parliamentarians.

West Stoke

Found as Stokes in a document dated 1205 and as Stoke juxta Cycestre 1288. Here Old English *stoc* refers to a 'special place', however, this should not be understood as anything religious, simply somewhere set aside for a specific purpose. The addition distinguishes this from North Stoke and South Stoke.

Wiggenholt

A name found as Wikeolte in 1195 and as Wygeholt in 1230, this is derived from a Saxon personal name and Old English *holt* and tells of 'the small wood or copse of a man called Wicga'.

Local names include Lickfold, from Old English *leac fald* which literally describes 'the pen where leeks are grown' but should be seen as referring to a kitchen garden. Much as Hoover has become the generic term for a vacuum cleaner, *leac* was once used as a general term for vegetables.

Wisborough Green

Listed as Wisebergh in 1227, this is from Old English *wisc beorg* and describes 'the hill by the marshy area'. The addition is from Middle English *grene* and refers to the village green'.

The suffix in Amblehurst is from *hyrst* 'the wooded hill of a man called Aemela', also seen in Brinkhurst Furze or 'the wooded hill of a man called Brynca', and in Dunhurst 'the hill with a woodland'. Headfoldswood Farm tells us it was 'the pen or fold associated with a man called Huda', Lowfold is 'the pen or fold of a man called Lulla', and Orfold Farm is from *ofer falod* 'the higher pen or fold'.

Barnfold is either *bern fold* 'the pen or enclosure near a barn' or, more likely, *bern feld* 'the open land with a barn'. Drungewick is 'the dairy farm of the family or followers of a man called Deora'. Gunshot Common is from *shud* 'the shed of a man called Guma'. A Saxon personal name and Old English *wudu* produce Loxwood, 'the wood of a man called Locc'. Shipbourne Farm is from *sceap burna* 'the stream near where sheep are grazed'.

Two names which are very specific. Pallingham Farm takes *ham inga* and tells of 'the homestead associated with the people of the place called Poling'. Beldhamland Farm talks of 'the *ham* or homestead of the beadle', telling us it was land used to raise money to pay for the upkeep of the official.

The Three Crowns public house does indeed have three crowns on its sign, this representing the unification of three kingdoms by James VI of Scotland becoming James I of England and Ireland. Both the Cricketers Arms and also the Bat and Ball show pubs were very aware of the importance of cricket to the community.

Wiston

From a Saxon personal name and Old English *tun*, this tells of 'the farmstead of a man called Wigstan or Winestan'. This name is listed as Wistanestun in the *Domesday* record of 1086.

Buddington is derived from a Saxon personal name and Old English *ing tun* and refers to 'the farmstead associated with a man called Buda'. Sevier's Barn has seen a slight change in spelling from what was a place associated with a man known as 'a maker of sieves'.

Wittering (East & West)

Two places with a common origin listed as Wihttringes in 683 and as Westringes in 1086, the later additions are self-explanatory. Here a Saxon personal name and Old English *inga* combine to tell of the '(place of) the family or followers of a man called Wihthere'.

Minor place names start with Bracklesham Farm, which started life as 'the homestead of a man called Braccol'; Cakeham is a similar name, hence a similar definition as 'the homestead of a man called Cacca'; Eleanor Farm is from 'the *ora* or bank of land associated with a man called Ealda'; Nunnington Farm reminds us it was 'the farmstead associated with a man called Nunna'; Redlands Farm informs us this was 'the cleared lands'; Somerley is easily seen as 'the woodland clearing used in summer months'; Stubcroft Farm can still be recognised as 'the smallholding by the stubbed trees', and Thorney Farm was settled as 'the dry ground in the marsh where thorn trees grow'.

Pub names include the Lamb Inn, a name with a religious connection for the Lamb of God was a reference to Jesus Christ. The Royal Oak has long been one of the most common names in the country, clearly this represents an important event and few schoolchildren will not have been told of the exploits of Charles II in which he hid in the branches of an oak tree to escape the parliamentarians who walked just feet below. The Shore Inn is on Shore Road, both a stone's throw from the coastline.

The Old House at Home is the title of a poem, where those fighting overseas reminisce on their childhood and associate it with the comforts of home.

Oh the old house at home where my forefathers dwelt

Where a child at the feet of my mother I knelt

Where she taught me the prayer, where she read me the page

Which, if infancy lisps, is the solace of age

My heart, 'mid the changes, wherever I roam

Ne'er loses its love for the old house at home

It became popular following the 19th-century poem written by Thomas Haynes Bayly being put to music by Edward Loder in the 1838 opera *Francis the First*. If this composition has never been heard of before, the review by the *Literary Gazette* of the opening night might explain why. 'The few public present thought it the most stupid piece of trash that ever disgraced the stage, in which opinion we entirely agree with them.' This did not stop this song becoming popular on both sides of the Atlantic.

Woodmancote

Here is a name found as Odemanscote in the *Domesday* record of 1086, and in a document dated 1240 as Wodemanecot. Here is a place name telling us it was 'the *cotes* or cottages of the woodmen'.

Locally we find Bilsborough Farm, this describing 'the *beorg* or hill of a man called Billa'. The local pub is the Wheatsheaf, an heraldic image used by both the Brewers' Company and the Worshipful Company of Bakers and probably an indication the landlord was both brewer and baker to the community.

Woolavington

This name in its present form first appears as Wellauenton in 1209, a name featuring a Saxon personal name with Old English *inga tun* to tell of 'the farmstead of the family or followers of a man called Wulflaf'.

Even earlier records of this name show it was formerly known as East Lavington, to distinguish it from West Lavington, a name discussed under its own entry. What appears to be the earlier name seems to show the personal name as 'Laf'. Yet personal names simply do not change from a pet or shortened form to the original. From this we can deduce the earlier records of East Lavington (and this also applies to West Lavington) are simply alternatives to the correct form. While West Lavington kept the corrupt form, in this example the original version was in regular use and the alternative eventually forgotten.

Woolbeding

Listed as Welbedlinge in the *Domesday* record of 1086, this is derived from a Saxon personal name and Old English *ing* and tells of the 'place associated with a man called Wulfbeald'.

Farthings did not refer to a rent but to 'a fourth part', something cut into four roughly equal parts. Indeed the farthing, a pre-decimal coin, has identical origins for before such were minted these were created by simply cutting the old penny into four. Redford is from *ridde ford* 'the river crossing by the cleared land', while Tyeland Farm informs us it was 'open common land'.

Worth

Found as Orbe in the *Domesday* record of 1086, this is hardly recognisable from the original Old English *worth* and describes 'the enclosure'.

Burleigh is easily seen as coming from *burh leah* 'the woodland clearing by the fortified place'. Cuttinglye Wood features a Saxon personal name and Old English *ing leah* to tell of 'the woodland clearing associated with a man called Cufela'. Kits Bridge was a place 'frequented by kites'. Rowfant describes 'the rough land covered by bracken'. Tiltwood tells us was 'the land under cultivation by the wood'. Three Bridges is a modern name, we can be sure as these bridges did not exist until the coming of the railways.

The local is the Parsons Pig, which seems to have no etymological value but was simply created as a pub name. It does put together an unexpected combination, while aliteration is always an advertising favourite.

Worthing

Listed as Ordinges in *Domesday*, this is a Saxon personal name and Old English *inga* and tells us this was the '(place of) the family or followers of a man called Weorth'.

Street names begin with Shelley Road, more likely to have been named after Sir Timothy Shelley than his son, the poet Percy. However, wordsmiths were certainly in mind when planners gave us neighbouring Milton Road, John Milton is best known for *Paradise Lost*; Wordsworth Road, remembers William Wordsworth whose major works include the *Lyrical Ballads* collection; the nursery rhyme *What are Little Boys Made of?* is among the lesser known works of Robert Southey who gave his name to Southey Road; Alfred, Lord Tennyson's list of works includes *The Charge of the Light Brigade* and is commemorated by Tennyson Road; while the Bard of Avon himself, William Shakespeare, who gave us the poem *All the World's a Stage* is remembered in Shakespeare Road.

Taking the name of Broadwater Street is the Broadwater public house, however, there is longer history here. Looking out to sea today the inlet which gave the name to centuries old 'broad water' silted up and disappeared in the 18th century. Looking inland from here we find a broken line of roads: The Steyne, a reminder of the former Steyne School; High Street, the most important street since the earliest days of the town, and Upper High Street; thereafter becoming Dagmar Street; then across the railway track to the footpath known as The Quashetts; Charmandean Lane, a reminder of the house here, demolished in 1963; and finally reaching the South Downs. This straight road would be easy to see as Roman, yet there is plenty of evidence to show this was here centuries before, adding weight to the increasing idea that many supposed 'Roman' roads are actually much older tracks expertly surfaced by the Empire.

Pub names of Worthing split into the various categories. Clearly to advertise the product required a little thought, especially when the vast majority were illiterate. The Jolly Brewers refers to both the product and the effect it would produce, or so they hoped. Wheatsheaf has links to brewing as it is an image found on the coat of arms of the Brewers' Company.

Not exactly the product but perhaps the menu is advertised by the Trout, a large pond behind the building providing fresh fish. The name of the Eden instantly brings to mind the biblical paradise, which may well have been the intention in suggesting this was the perfect place to relax. However, the invitation is even more obvious when naming another establishment the Rest.

Location was in mind when naming the Toad at Press House, this building has had several uses before becoming a pub at the end of the second millenium.

Anyone who remembers the nursery rhyme character will hardly be surprised to find the Jack Horner on a corner. Appropriately the Half Brick was built in an area which was once brick fields.

The Smugglers Return was never the abode of any dealer in contraband, especially not the lifesize pirate-type figure standing outside, this is simply a predictable link to the sea. A Town's Pride is how the people of Worthing referred to the lifeboatmen, it not only producing a pub name but also a book by Rob Blann.

The Rose and Crown show this was run by a patriot, the rose representing the nation and the crown its monarch. The other great power in the land is also represented in pub names, although the church may not seem to have much in common with pubs today. Landlords would often show their religious beliefs in a subtle way, such as the likely Catholic who named his pub the Bull as the papal bull is named for the seal on the pope's edicts.

That the Swan Inn is on the high street is a likely indication this is derived from an heraldic image rather than the bird. The Selden Arms features the coat of arms of a family associated with the county since the 13th century. The Hare and Hounds originated as a reference to the sport of hare coursing. Banned in the UK in 2004 (coming into force in February 2005), it was designed to test the skills of the dogs to run, overtake and turn the hare. However, its popularity dived with the introduction of greyhound racing.

Among the popular figures commemorated here are Thomas Becket, a local school also known by his name. Born in London in 1117, he was chancellor, adviser and close friend of Henry II, who rose to become Archbishop of Canterbury. It has been suggested their friendship had deteriorated to the point where Henry ordered his knights to kill him with the famous line 'Who will rid me of this turbulent priest?' but this is unlikely to be proven either way. We do know he was murdered and in the cathedral at Canterbury, too, where the site is now a shrine in Geoffrey Chaucer's *Canterbury Tales*. All these factors have made St Thomas a Becket arguably still the most famous Archbishop of Canterbury in history. Better known than the 80 or so who followed him and more than 800 years after his death.

Sir Timothy Shelley, 2nd Baronet of Castle Goring (1753–1844) may not be the first name which comes to mind, especially not when thinking of a pub name. He entered the House of Commoms as member of parliament for Shoreham, living at Warnham where he fathered six children. The eldest was Percy Bysshe Shelley, his middle name from his paternal grandfather, the English Romantic poet who died 22 years before his father.

Another wordsmith, Charles Dickens, should probably have had more pubs named to honour him as his fame is probably only second to William Shakespeare as an English writer of yesteryear. The Richard Cobden remembers a local 19th-century man who was a leading businessman and radical Liberal statesman. He founded the Anti-Corn Law League and was a leading light in seeking peace to increase trade.

The Montague Arms recalls Anthony Browne, 1st Viscount Montague, whose family were lords of the manor of Worthing for more than two centuries. The Neville family, earls of Warwick, have been major landowners throughout much of English history, hence the name of the Warwick Arms. The Egremont Hotel bears the arms of the Rt Hon George O'Brien Wyndham, Earl of Egremont. The Duke of Connaught and Stratheam was a title held by the Earl of Essex, Prince William, son of Queen Victoria and the inspiration for the name of the Connaught public house.

Ye John Seldon was named after the man whose surname was actually Selden and who lived from 1584 to 1654. Born at Salvington, he is remembered as a jurist and scholar of English law, the constitution, and ancient Jewish law. Not surprisingly the Corner House is on a sharp corner. The Maple Leaf may have been named for the Canadian troops based in Sussex. The Cissbury Tap is named after Cissbury Ring, an ancient earthwork some distance north of Worthing.

The Southdown Hotel tells us where the place is located, on the lower slopes of the south downs, the Downlands has the same meaning. The Dolphin is another reminder of the location as this mammal is associated with the sea and regarded as a friend to mariners. Ye Olde House At Home recalls the poem set to music and telling of how the soldier serving his country overseas yearns for his youth and the comfort of home. The Elms takes the name of the prominent nearby trees. Wigmore Road gives a name to the Wigmore public house.

The Royal Oak is one of the most common pub names in the land. This originates in the famous exploits of Charles II who, as virtually every schoolchild learned in their history lesson, hid in an oak tree to escape Parliamentarians following defeat at the Battle of Worcester in 1651. Yet such a name, and the reasons behind it, has not only been used for pub names but also for eight ships of the Royal Navy. Indeed the use of this with a royal connection is probably more appropriate as the name of a ship, from 1664, than of a pub, from 1660. The sign is one of the far too few examples of a double-image, on one side the vessel seen sailing stormy waters, while on the reverse it is on the calmest of seas. This is undoubtedly HMS *Royal Oak*, a Prince Consort class vessel launched on 10 September 1862.

While the switch from wooden sailing ships to propeller-driven metal-hulled vessels was comparatively quick, the HMS *Royal Oak* was one of the few built to have both fitted. The propeller could be hoisted out of the water to prevent drag when under sail, however, most often it was simply disengaged from the engine. It seems likely the propeller was hoisted clear of the water on 9 February 1864 for, while *en route* from Gibraltar to Malta, it achieved a speed of 13.5 knots. This is the only recorded occasion a vessel with both modes of power ever achieved a greater speed under sail than theoretically capable of mechanically.

Y

Yapton

Recorded as Abbiton around the end of the 12th century, here is a Saxon personal name and Old English *ing tun*, referring to 'the farmstead associated with a man called Eabba'.

Bisham is a local name which was once an independent settlement known as 'the *ham* of a man called Byli'.

The Maypole Inn conjures up an image of a traditional springtime on the village green, which is exactly where this name originates. The Olive Branch reminds us of the story of Noah's Ark, the dove returning and indicating the flood waters were receding; it probably suggested itself as a pub name from the arms of the Shipwrights' Company. During the coaching era one of the delicacies found on the menu in Sussex pubs, also lent itself to the name of the Shoulder of Mutton and Cucumbers.

Common Place Name Elements

Element	Origin	Meaning
ac	Old English	oak tree
banke	Old Scandinavian	bank, hill slope
bearu	Old English	grove, wood
bekkr	Old Scandinavian	stream
berg	Old Scandinavian	hill
birce	Old English	birch tree
brad	Old English	broad
broc	Old English	brook, stream
brycg	Old English	bridge
burh	Old English	fortified place
burna	Old English	stream
by	Old Scandinavian	farmstead
ceap	Old English	market
ceaster	Old English	Roman stronghold
cirice	Old English	church
clif	Old English	cliff, slope
cocc	Old English	woodcock
cot	Old English	cottage
cumb	Old English	valley
cweorn	Old English	queorn
cyning	Old English	king
dael	Old English	valley
dalr	Old Scandinavian	valley
denu	Old English	valley
draeg	Old English	portage

dun	Old English	hill
ea	Old English	river
east	Old English	east
ecg	Old English	edge
eg	Old English	island
eorl	Old English	nobleman
eowestre	Old English	fold for sheep
ersc	Old English	wooded hill
fald	Old English	animal enclosure
feld	Old English	open land
ford	Old English	river crossing
ful	Old English	foul, dirty
geard	Old English	yard
geat	Old English	gap, pass
haeg	Old English	enclosure
haeth	Old English	heath
haga	Old English	hedged enclosure
halh	Old English	nook of land
ham	Old English	homestead
hamm	Old English	river meadow
heah	Old English	high, chief
hlaw	Old English	tumulus, mound
hoh	Old English	hill spur
hop	Old English	enclosed valley
hrycg	Old English	ridge
hwaete	Old English	wheat
hwit	Old English	white
hyll	Old English	hill

lacu	Old English	stream, water course
lang	Old English	long
langr	Old Scandinavian	long
leah	Old English	woodland clearing
lytel	Old English	little
meos	Old English	moss
mere	Old English	lake
middel	Old English	middle
mor	Old English	moorland
myln	Old English	mill
niwe	Old English	new
north	Old English	north
ofer	Old English	bank, ridge
pol	Old English	pool, pond
preost	Old English	priest
ruh	Old English	rough
salh	Old English	willow
sceaga	Old English	small wood, copse
sceap	Old English	sheep
stan	Old English	stone, boundary stone
steinn	Old Scandinavian	stone, boundary stone
stapol	Old English	post, pillar
stoc	Old English	secondary or special settlement
stocc	Old English	stump, log
stow	Old English	assembly or holy place
straet	Old English	Roman road
suth	Old English	south
thorp	Old Scandinavian	outlying farmstead

treow	Old English	tree, post
tun	Old English	farmstead
wald	Old English	woodland, forest
wella	Old English	spring, stream
west	Old English	west
wic	Old English	specialised, usually dairy farm
withig	Old English	willow tree
worth	Old English	an enclosure
wudu	Old English	wood

Bibliography

Barlow, Sylvia *Horsham Streets* (The History Press, 2007)

Bognor Regis Local History Society *A Brief Guide to Places of Interest* (1981)

Dunkling, Leslie and Wright, Gordon *A Dictionary of Pub Names* (Routledge & Kegan Paul, 1987)

Ekwall, Eilert *The Concise Oxford Dictionary of English Place Names* (Oxford University Press, 1960)

Green, Kenneth *The Street Names of Chichester*

Jerrome, Peter *Tread Lightly Here* (Window Press, 1990)

Kerridge, R.G. *A History of Lancing* (Phillimore & Co. Ltd)

Magilton, John *Midhurst* (Chichester District Council 2001)

Mawer, A. and Stenton, F.M. *The Place Names of Sussex Pts I & II* (Cambridge, 1969)

Mills, A.D. *Dictionary of English Place Names* (Oxford, 1998)

The Shoreham-by-Sea History Portal